FAILURE
IS NOT MY
INHERITANCE

*Adversity to Purpose-Nurturing
Love and Success*

WRITTEN BY
DANIEL SELAPA

Copyrights

 FIRST PUBLISHED IN 2024 BY:
Ava'spublishers (Pty) Ltd

EMAIL: Books@avaspublishers.co.za
WEBSITES: www.avaspublishers.co.za
MOBILE NUMBER: +27796299733

Failure Is Not My Inheritance

From Adversity To Purpose-nurturing Love and Success

ISBN NUMBER: 978-0-7961-6090-4
Copyrights©2024Daniel Selapa

Edited by: Charles Hoby
  Sally Mabasa
  Puleng Mokhobo
Cover design by: Charles Hoby
Formatting & Typesetting by: Charles Hoby

All rights reserved, no part of this publication may be reproduced, stored in a retrieval system, transmitted, or utilized in any form or by any means, electronic, mechanical, photocopying, recording, or otherwise, without the prior permission of the author.

Printing and Binding by:

Groep 7 Drukkers en Uitgewers
www.groep7.co.za

Contents

Acknowledgements..i
Introduction...iii
Chapter 1: *The Absence of a Father*........................2
Chapter 2 : *The Negative Impact of a Lack of Education*..............8
Chapter 3 : *Finding Guidance in Unexpected Places*.................11
Chapter 4 : *Lessons from the Elders*...........................15
Chapter 5 : *Learning Responsibility*..........................18
Chapter 6 : *Climbing the Ladder of Hard Work*................21
Chapter 7 : *Overcoming Poverty*..............................25
Chapter 8 : *Passing It On*......................................29
Chapter 9 : *Inheritance of Love and Loss*....................33
Chapter 10 : *Failure Is Not an Option*.......................36
Chapter 11 : *The Legacy of Resilience*......................40
Chapter 12 : *The Uncharted Path*............................43
Chapter 13 : *"From Sales Apprentice to Entrepreneurial Visionary"*..............47
Chapter 14 : *In the Hallowed Halls of My School*...........50
Chapter 15 : *The Legacy of a Boychild's Journey*...........48
Chapter 16 : *The Guiding Hand of Faith*....................55
Chapter 17 : *A Life of Independence*........................58
Chapter 18 : *Leaving a Legacy of Faith*......................60
Chapter 19 : *The Heart of the Journey: A Mother's Love*..........62
Chapter 20 : *A Legacy of Love and Faith*...................65
Chapter 21 : *Brotherhood and Redemption*.................67
Chapter 22 : *The Journey of Two Brothers*.................70
Chapter 23 : *Lessons Learnt*..................................72
Chapter 24 : *Triumph Over Adversity: The Power of Unity*..........74
Chapter 25 : *A Testament to God's Love*....................77
Chapter 26 : *"Divine Intervention: A Taste of Grace"*.................79
Chapter 27 : *"A Test of Faith: Surrendering to the Divine"*..........83
Chapter 28 : *The Shadow of Absentee Parenting*..................87

Chapter 29 : *The Journey into Fatherhood*..................................90
Chapter 30 : *Navigating the Challenges of Fatherhood*................93
Chapter 31 : *Guiding Teenagers Through the Reckless Years*.......96
Chapter 32 : *Lessons from My Father's Legacy*..........................102
Chapter 33 : *Building Resilience for the Future*.........................105
Chapter 34 : *Navigating Disadvantages with Resilience*.............107
Chapter 35 : *Rising Stronger*...110
Chapter 36 : *The Therapeutic Power of Art*...............................112
Chapter 37 : *Art as an Escape from Self-Harm*.........................115
Chapter 38 : *Embracing the Healing Process*...........................117
Chapter 39 : *Inspiring Others Through Art*...............................119
Chapter 40 : *Lessons for Aspiring Men*....................................121
Chapter 41 : *Building Healthy Foundations*..............................129
Chapter 42 : *"Favour, Purpose, and the Divine Gift of Marriage"*...133
Chapter 43 : *Communication and Connection*..........................136
Chapter 44 : *Empathy and Understanding*................................149
Chapter 45 : *The Cornerstones of Love*....................................159
Chapter 46 : *Conflict Resolution and Growth*............................163
Chapter 47 : *Nurturing Lifelong Love*.......................................169
Chapter 48 : *Breaking the Chains of Misconception*..................171
Chapter 49 : *Lessons in Love and Interdependence*..................173
Chapter 50 : *Independence and Beyond: Success without Disadvantage*..175
Chapter 51 : *Breaking the Chains of Misconception*..................166
Chapter 52 : *Lessons in Love and Interdependence*...................179
Chapter 53 : *Independence and Beyond: Success Without Disadvantage*..181
Chapter 54 : *"Nurturing True Love and Success: My Journey"*....183
Chapter 55 : *The Weight of Generational Curses*......................187
Chapter 56 : *Failure Is Not My Inheritance*...............................193
Biography of the Author..195

Acknowledgements

Writing a book is never a solitary journey, and I am deeply grateful to the many individuals who have supported and inspired me along the way. First and foremost, I want to express my heartfelt gratitude to my family for their unwavering love, encouragement, and understanding throughout this endeavour. Your belief in me has been my guiding light, and I am forever grateful for your endless support.

To all the individuals I have had the privilege to lead and manage throughout my career, thank you for your dedication, hard work, and unwavering commitment. Your resilience and passion have inspired me every day, and it has been an honour to work alongside each of you. Special thanks to KM Mashaba, the school principal, for entrusting Comrade with crafting the speech "Failure is not my inheritance," which ultimately influenced the title of this book. Your support and trust have played a significant role in shaping my path.

I am indebted to my teachers, colleagues, and friends who have shared their knowledge, insights, and experiences with me. Your generosity and camaraderie have enriched my life in countless ways, and I am honoured to have crossed paths with each of you.

I would like to extend a heartfelt thank you to the great church of St. Engenas ZCC and its elders for becoming my mentors. Your guidance and wisdom have been invaluable in my journey of self-discovery and growth. I am forever grateful to my late aunt, Kwena Salome Matlala, for stepping into the role of my stepmother and always standing by me. Your love and support have helped shape me into the person I am today. To Mam Mmethi, who opened the doors for me to run my automotive business without paying rent, I am deeply thankful for your generosity and belief in my potential.

A special mention goes to my daughter, Tumelo Rorisang, whose presence in my life has pushed me to take bigger steps and strive for greatness. Your love and encouragement have been a constant source of motivation.

Last but not least, I want to express my deepest gratitude to my mother, the pillar of my strength, who has always had my back and encouraged me to keep going, no matter the obstacles.

To my readers, thank you for embarking on this journey with me. Your support and encouragement have fuelled my passion for storytelling, and I am humbled by the opportunity to share my experiences with you.

To all the individuals who have contributed to this book's creation, from editors and designers to publishing professionals, thank you for your dedication and expertise. Your efforts have brought this project to life, and I am deeply thankful for your hard work and commitment. With heartfelt appreciation, KAMOGELO DANIEL SELAPA.

Introduction

In the dimly lit room of my childhood, I learned a profound lesson: that failure is not my inheritance. Growing up without a father, I faced a world filled with uncertainty and hardships, but I refused to let those define me. This book is the chronicle of my journey, from the darkness of poverty and lack of education to the light of knowledge, responsibility, and hard work.

CHAPTER 1

Chapter 1

✢ *The Absence of a Father*

Short Story: A lonely boy's journey begins in a world without a father's guidance.

In the dimly lit room of my childhood, where the shadows seemed to dance with the flickering candlelight, I began a journey marked by the profound absence of a father's guidance. It was a journey that would shape the course of my life in ways I could scarcely comprehend at that tender age.

As a young boy, the void left by my absent father was palpable, like a missing puzzle piece that left the picture incomplete. I yearned for his presence, for the reassuring hand on my shoulder, and for the wisdom only a father could impart. But, as fate would have it, he was taken from us when I was just eight years old, leaving behind a family in turmoil.

My father's absence was not just physical; it cast a long shadow over our household. It was as if the walls of our home held echoes of his laughter, his stern advice, and the comforting embrace that only a father could provide. In his absence, my mother became the pillar of our family, a role she embraced with unwavering determination.

The impact of this void was felt in a myriad of ways. I found myself wrestling with questions about what it meant to be a man. I saw other boys with fathers who taught them life's essential lessons—how to tie a tie, how to stand tall in the face of adversity, and how to navigate the complexities of this world. I, on the other hand, had to piece together these lessons on my own, often through trial and error.

But it was in those early years, amidst the uncertainty and longing that I began to grasp the essence of resilience. I learned that life does not always adhere to our plans, that adversity can be a relentless companion, and that sometimes the absence of a guiding hand can be the catalyst for our own self-discovery.

In the chapters that follow, I will recount the remarkable journey that took me from the depths of poverty and a lack of education to the heights of knowledge, responsibility, and hard work. Through these words, I hope to inspire others who have faced similar challenges, showing them that the absence of a father need not define their destinies. For, as I came to realise, failure is not my inheritance.

Advice: The void left by an absent father can be filled with mentors, teachers, and positive role models. Seek them out.

Lesson: Life's challenges can be overcome with the right support and determination.

As I reflect on the remarkable journey that has brought me from the depths of poverty and a lack of education to the heights of knowledge, responsibility, and hard work, I am reminded of the words of the elders: "Your story can inspire others to change their lives." It is with this conviction that I recount the chapters of my life, with the hope of inspiring others who have faced similar challenges to see that the absence of a father need not define their destinies and that failure is not their inheritance.

The journey began in a small home in Seshego Zone 8, Polokwane, where I was raised by my single mother after the loss of my father at the tender age of eight. It was a modest home, and financial struggles were a constant companion. But it was within the walls of that home that the seeds of resilience and determination were sown.

My early years were marked by the absence of a father figure, and the weight of that absence was palpable. But within the community and the embrace of the church, I found unexpected sources of guidance and mentorship. The church elders, with their wrinkled faces and wisdom earned through a lifetime of experience, became my mentors and surrogate fathers. They instilled in me the importance of responsibility, the power of listening, and the value of respecting one's elders.

My pursuit of education was relentless, even when access to higher learning seemed uncertain. The financial constraints that shadowed my journey were met with a refusal to give up. I discovered unconventional routes to learning, embracing self-education, and challenging the notion that formal instruction was the sole path to knowledge. It was a time of resourcefulness and unwavering belief in the transformative power of education.

Hard work became my constant companion as I climbed the ladder of success. The pursuit of my dreams demanded sacrifices and unwavering dedication. It was in the moments of fatigue and doubt that I remembered the counsel of the elders, who had taught me that success was earned through effort and resilience. Every setback became a stepping stone, and every challenge was a test of my determination.

The weight of poverty that had hung over my family for generations was gradually lifted as I broke free from its suffocating grip. Education, hard work, and an unwavering belief in the power to change one's circumstances became the tools that dismantled the cycle of poverty. It was a journey that taught me that poverty was a circumstance, not a destiny.

The joy of helping others escape the clutches of poverty became a guiding principle in my life. I learned that success was most meaningful when shared, and I used my resources and knowledge to uplift others. It was a reminder that the true measure of success lay in the impact one had on the lives of others and that our stories could inspire change in the world.

As I look back on this remarkable journey, I am reminded that failure is not my inheritance. It is a journey marked by resilience, determination, and the unwavering belief that adversity can be transformed into opportunity. My hope is that these words will serve as a source of inspiration for others who face challenges, so that they may see that their destinies are not defined by the absence of a father and that failure is not their inheritance. For in the chapters of our lives, it is our stories that can inspire the greatest change.

The Struggle for Higher Education

The struggle to access higher education was a defining chapter in my life, one that would ultimately become a turning point. It led me on a journey of discovery, teaching me to find unconventional routes to learning, to embrace the value of self-education, and to challenge the notion that a lack of formal instruction should limit one's pursuit of knowledge and personal growth.

From a young age, I had harboured a deep thirst for knowledge. I was acutely aware of the transformative power of education and the doors it could open. However, the financial constraints that shadowed my family meant that the path to higher education was fraught with challenges.

My mother, a single parent with limited resources, had always emphasized the importance of education. She instilled in me the belief that it was the key to a brighter future. Yet, as the time came to consider pursuing higher education, the barriers seemed insurmountable.

I vividly remember the day I received my matric results in 2017 from Peter Nchabeleng Secondary School. It was a moment filled with pride and hope, but it was also a moment when the reality of my circumstances hit home. I longed to further my studies, to delve deeper into the realms of knowledge, but the financial burden of tuition fees and living expenses loomed like an impenetrable wall.

Despite the odds, I refused to relinquish my dreams. It was during this period of uncertainty that I discovered unconventional routes to learning. I scoured libraries, seeking out books on a wide array of subjects. I became a regular visitor at the local library, spending hours immersed in books on science, literature, and history. It was a form of self-education that allowed me to expand my horizons and acquire knowledge outside the confines of formal instruction.

The elders in my community became my allies in this quest for knowledge. They shared their own experiences of pursuing education through unconventional means, recounting tales of resilience and resourcefulness. They encouraged me to see that education was not limited to the classroom and that the world was a vast repository of knowledge waiting to be explored.

In challenging the notion that formal instruction was the only path to education, I embarked on a journey of self-discovery. I dove into online courses, tapping into the vast wealth of information available on the internet. It was a period of self-guided learning where I sought out courses, articles, and resources that would help me acquire the knowledge I craved.

The struggle for higher education taught me that determination and resourcefulness could bridge the gap between dreams and reality. It was a turning point that reshaped my perspective on education and personal growth. In the absence of formal instruction, I had discovered that the pursuit of knowledge knew no bounds.

This chapter stands as a testament to the resilience of the human spirit and our unwavering belief in the power of education. It is a reminder that, even in the face of seemingly insurmountable obstacles, the pursuit of knowledge can be a transformative journey, one that leads to unexpected discoveries and personal growth.

Reflection Question: How has the absence of a father figure in your life influenced your journey?

Exercise: Write a letter to your younger self, offering guidance and support that you wish you had received.

CHAPTER 2

Chapter 2

✣ *The Negative Impact of a Lack of Education*

Short Story: A young mind hungry for knowledge but lacking proper education
: The Struggle to Access Higher Education

My high school graduation should have been a moment of celebration, a culmination of years of hard work and dedication. Yet, it marked the beginning of a new challenge: the struggle to access higher education. While I had completed my high school journey, the path to further instruction was fraught with obstacles.

As I stood on the precipice of adulthood, the absence of a father and the lack of proper guidance weighed heavily on my shoulders. The dream of pursuing a higher education burned brightly within me, but the financial constraints and limited opportunities loomed like insurmountable barriers.

I watched as my peers, armed with acceptance letters and scholarships, embarked on their journeys to institutions of higher learning. Their futures seemed to stretch out before them, paved with the promise of knowledge and opportunity. Meanwhile, I found myself at a crossroads, wondering if my dreams of a higher education would remain just that—dreams.

This chapter delves into the challenges I faced during this pivotal period of my life. It explores the financial hardships that often accompany the pursuit of higher education, the limited access to scholarships and financial aid, and the emotional toll of feeling left behind. It's a chapter that resonates with countless individuals who have yearned for a chance at higher learning but found themselves constrained by circumstances beyond their control.

But it's also a chapter of resilience and resourcefulness. It showcases the determination to overcome these obstacles, to find alternative pathways to education, and to refuse to be defined by the limitations imposed by financial constraints. It's a chapter that reflects the unwavering belief that education is not a privilege but a fundamental right and that with persistence, opportunities can be uncovered even in the face of adversity.

In the chapters that follow, I will recount how this struggle to access higher education became a turning point in my life. It led me to discover unconventional routes to learning, to embrace the value of self-education, and to challenge the notion that a lack of formal instruction should limit one's pursuit of knowledge and personal growth.

Advice: Never underestimate the power of self-education. Books and mentors can be your greatest teachers.

Lesson: Education is the key that unlocks the doors to a better future.

Reflection Question: What barriers to education have you faced, and how have they shaped your perspective?

Exercise: Create a vision board that represents your educational and personal growth goals.

CHAPTER 3

Chapter 3

✛ *Finding Guidance in Unexpected Places*

Short Story: Discovering a group of elders at the church who became unexpected mentors.
: *Finding Guidance in Unexpected Places*

In the heart of my tumultuous journey, a glimmer of hope emerged, like a beacon cutting through the darkest night. It was a chapter of my life where I discovered guidance in the most unexpected of places: a group of elders within the sanctuary of our church who would become my mentors and pillars of strength.

As I grappled with the challenges of navigating a world without a father and the hurdles of limited education, it was within the walls of our local church that I found solace. The dimly lit pews, the scent of polished wood, and the hushed whispers of prayers became the backdrop of my transformative experiences.

It was in this sacred space that I encountered a group of wise elders, individuals whose life experiences and deep spiritual insights would become an unexpected wellspring of guidance. These individuals had weathered the storms of life, and their wrinkled faces held the stories of triumph over adversity. They became my mentors, offering not just spiritual guidance but also invaluable life lessons.

In this chapter, I will share the profound impact these mentors had on my journey. They became the compass that pointed me in the right direction when I felt lost. Their counsel extended far beyond matters of faith; they imparted wisdom on responsibility, perseverance, and the importance of community.

I will recount the stories of these remarkable individuals, each with their own unique life journeys and perspectives. They became surrogate fathers, offering the guidance and support I longed for in the absence of my own. They taught me valuable lessons about navigating life's challenges with grace and humility.

This chapter serves as a testament to the unexpected sources of strength and wisdom that can illuminate our paths during the darkest of times. It is a reminder that guidance and mentorship can come from the most unlikely of places, and that sometimes, the individuals who shape our destinies are those we least expect.

In the chapters that follow, I will delve deeper into the life lessons I gleaned from these remarkable elders, lessons that would serve as the building blocks of my journey from adversity to purpose.

Advice: Be open to guidance from people who genuinely care about your well-being.

Lesson: Wisdom can come from the most unexpected sources.

Surrogate Fathers: Wisdom from Unexpected Sources

This chapter is a tribute to the remarkable individuals who played the role of surrogate fathers in my life, offering guidance and support that I longed for in the absence of my own. Their stories, each marked by unique life journeys and perspectives, illuminated my path during some of the darkest times. They taught me invaluable lessons about navigating life's challenges with grace and humility.

Within the close-knit community of Seshego Zone 8, Polokwane, there were elders whose wisdom transcended their years. These were individuals whose faces bore the marks of time, etched with the lines of experiences that had shaped them into reservoirs of knowledge. To me, they were more than just community members; they became beacons of hope and mentors.

Their willingness to share their life stories was a gift that enriched my journey. Each of them had faced their own trials and tribulations, and their stories resonated with authenticity. They spoke of overcoming adversity, of persevering in the face of insurmountable odds, and of the importance of resilience.

One of these remarkable elders was Pastor LESESE, a man whose quiet strength and humility left an indelible mark on my character. He had faced significant hardships in his youth but had emerged from those trials with a deep sense of grace and resilience. His counsel was simple yet profound: "Life will test you, my child, but it is in how you respond to those tests that your character is revealed."

Another surrogate father figure was MR. MABOTHA, a teacher whose love for learning was contagious. He shared stories of his own struggles to access education, and it was through his guidance that I developed a deep appreciation for the pursuit of knowledge. His mantra, "Education is the key to unlocking your future," echoed in my mind as I forged my unconventional path to learning.

The elders taught me the importance of listening more than I spoke, a lesson that would prove invaluable in the years to come. They emphasized that wisdom often lay in silence, in the moments when we absorbed the experiences and insights of those who had walked the path before us.

Respect for one's elders became a foundational principle instilled in me through their guidance. They emphasized that humility was the key to growth and that the wisdom of age deserved reverence. It was a lesson that transcended generational divides and underscored the importance of intergenerational mentorship.

Reflection Question: Who are the unexpected mentors or guides in your life, and what have they taught you?

Exercise: Reach out to one of your mentors and express your gratitude for their influence.

CHAPTER 4

Chapter 4

✢ *Lessons from the Elders*

Short Story: A collection of wisdom imparted by the church elders.
Lessons from the Elders

Within the hallowed halls of our church, I had the privilege of being a student of life, learning invaluable lessons from a group of elders whose wisdom flowed as steadily as a timeless river. This chapter is a collection of the profound teachings imparted by these venerable mentors, each nugget of wisdom a precious gem that illuminated my path.

Short Story: A Collection of Wisdom

The elders of our church formed a council of sages whose knowledge transcended the confines of books and classrooms. Their wisdom was born from the crucible of life itself, and they generously shared it with a young, eager soul like mine. Gathered around after Sunday services or during weekday gatherings, they offered insights that were more precious than gold.

Their stories were a tapestry of human experiences, interwoven with triumphs and tribulations, joys and sorrows. With each tale they told, I was transported to different epochs of history, learning not just about their lives but about the collective wisdom of generations.

Advice: Listen more than you speak

One of the first and most enduring lessons from the elders was the art of listening. They taught me that wisdom often resides in silence, in the spaces between words. In a world where voices clamour for attention, the ability to listen attentively is a rare and valuable skill.

They shared stories of their own journeys, emphasizing how the act of listening had guided them through life's labyrinthine twists and turns. They taught me that by listening to others, we gain not only knowledge but also empathy, compassion, and a deeper understanding of the human condition.

Lesson: Respect for Your Elders

Respect for one's elders, they insisted, was the cornerstone of wisdom. This respect was not merely a matter of etiquette; it was a profound recognition of the reservoir of knowledge that older generations hold. The elders recounted the days when they, too, were young and headstrong, often dismissing the advice of their elders. With time, they had come to realize the profound truth that youth benefit greatly from the guidance of experience.

In this chapter, I will share these pearls of wisdom with you, the readers, in the hope that they may resonate with your own journeys. The lessons I learned from the church elders transcend time and circumstance, offering universal truths that can guide us all towards lives of purpose, understanding, and reverence for the wisdom that surrounds us. Their teachings continue to shape my path, and I hope they will do the same for you.

Reflection Question: What wisdom have you gained from older individuals in your life, and how have you applied it?

Exercise: Interview an elder in your family or community and document their life experiences.

CHAPTER 5

Chapter 5

Learning Responsibility

Short Story: The moment when I realized that being responsible was the path to a better life.

Learning Responsibility

In the tumultuous journey of my life, there came a pivotal moment, like a beam of light piercing through the darkness, when I realized that embracing responsibility was the path to a better life. This chapter chronicles that transformative moment and the lessons it carried.

Short Story: The Moment of Realisation

Responsibility had always been a concept that danced at the periphery of my awareness. I had observed the elders in my community—those who shoulder the burdens of their families and communities with grace and determination. But it wasn't until a specific moment that its true significance came into focus.

It was an ordinary day, one of those unremarkable snapshots in the album of life. I stood at a crossroads, facing a decision that would have far-reaching consequences. It was in that moment of choice that responsibility revealed itself as the linchpin of my destiny. I chose to step up, to take ownership of my actions, and in that choice, I began to understand the profound impact it could have.

Advice: Take Ownership of Your Actions

The elders in my community have always emphasized the importance of taking ownership of one's actions. They taught me that responsibility begins with the recognition that our choices have consequences, both for ourselves and for those around us. By acknowledging our role in shaping our destinies, we gain agency over our lives.

They shared stories of their own journeys, highlighting the moments when they faced crucial decisions and the importance of taking responsibility for the outcomes, whether positive or negative. They imparted the wisdom that true growth occurs when we are willing to confront the consequences of our actions and use them as stepping stones to progress.

Lesson: Responsibility is the Seed of Success

Through their teachings, I came to understand that responsibility is not merely a burden but a seed from which success can grow. It is the foundation upon which character is built and the cornerstone of achievement. The elders showed me that by embracing responsibility, we demonstrate our commitment to growth, to self-improvement, and to contributing positively to our communities.

This chapter is a testament to the transformative power of responsibility. It's a reminder that every choice we make and every action we take is an opportunity to exercise responsibility and shape our destinies. In the pages that follow, I will delve deeper into how this pivotal realization propelled me towards a path of purpose and accomplishment and how it can do the same for anyone willing to embrace it.

Reflection Question: How has taking responsibility for your actions transformed your life?

Exercise: Create a list of three responsibilities you want to focus on in your life and set achievable goals for each.

CHAPTER 6

CHAPTER 6

Climbing the Ladder of Hard Work

Short Story: The relentless pursuit of my dreams through hard work.

Climbing the Ladder of Hard Work

Within the chapters of my life, there emerged a phase characterized by the relentless pursuit of my dreams through unwavering hard work. Chapter 6 encapsulates this journey of determination, offering a glimpse into the sacrifices made and the lessons learned along the way.

Short Story: The Relentless Pursuit of Dreams

Dreams had always beckoned to me like distant stars in the night sky—enticing but seemingly out of reach. But I had learned from the elders that success was not a gift bestowed upon anyone; it was earned through unwavering effort. With this conviction burning in my heart, I embarked on a journey marked by relentless hard work.

It was a journey that often demanded more of me than I thought possible. Days turned into nights as I poured over books, honed my skills, and pushed myself beyond the limits of fatigue. There were moments of doubt when the weight of my aspirations threatened to overwhelm me, but I pressed on.

Advice: Success is Earned Through Effort

The elders had instilled in me the belief that success was a reward for those who were willing to put in the effort. They shared stories of their own toil and perseverance, of the times when they had labored tirelessly to achieve their goals. Their counsel was clear: success was not a matter of chance but a consequence of hard work.

They emphasized the importance of diligence, consistency, and resilience. They taught me that, in the pursuit of dreams, setbacks and obstacles were inevitable. But it was through unwavering effort and an unyielding spirit that these obstacles could be overcome.

Lesson: Hard Work is the Bridge to Reality

Through their guidance, I came to understand that hard work was the bridge that connected dreams to reality. It was the labour of hands and the sweat of brows that transformed aspirations into achievements. The elders had shown me that every ounce of effort I invested was a step forward on the path to success.

This chapter stands as a testament to the transformative power of hard work, and it serves as a reminder that dreams are not fulfilled by wishful thinking but by the determined labour of those who dare to pursue them. In the pages that follow, I will delve deeper into how my unwavering commitment to hard work propelled me towards my goals and how it can do the same for anyone willing to put in the effort.

One of the key lessons I learned about hard work was that it was not limited to a specific time or place. It was a way of life, a mindset that dictated my approach to every task. The church elders, with their stories of toil and perseverance, instilled in me the belief that there were no shortcuts on the path to success.

The pursuit of knowledge required a steadfast commitment to hard work. In the absence of formal education, I turned to self-guided learning and devoured books, online courses, and educational resources with unbridled enthusiasm. It was a laborious journey, marked by countless hours of study and reflection.

Hard work was not solely about quantity but also about quality. I learned that it was not enough to merely put in long hours; I had to ensure that my efforts were purposeful and directed towards my goals. The elders' stories of their own work ethics, whether in farming, teaching, or other professions, underscored the importance of diligence and excellence in one's endeavours.

One of the most valuable aspects of hard work was its ability to build character. It taught me discipline, resilience, and perseverance. It was in moments of exhaustion and doubt that I discovered reservoirs of inner strength I never knew existed. Hard work had the power to mold me into a person of substance, someone capable of overcoming challenges with grace.

Hard work also allowed me to bridge the gap between dreams and reality. It was the bridge that connected my aspirations to tangible achievements. Through relentless effort, I began to see my goals materialize, whether in the form of academic achievements, career milestones, or personal growth.

As I reflect on this chapter of my life, I am reminded that hard work is not a solitary endeavour. It is a force that connects us to the legacies of those who came before us as well as to the aspirations of future generations. It is a reminder that, in the pursuit of our dreams, we stand on the shoulders of those who worked tirelessly to pave the way.

Reflection Question: In what ways has hard work been a bridge to your dreams?

Exercise: Write down three long-term goals and the specific steps you plan to take to achieve them through hard work.

CHAPTER 7

CHAPTER 7

🞣 *Overcoming Poverty*

Short Story: Breaking free from the shackles of poverty through dedication and persistence

: Overcoming Poverty

In the tapestry of my life, Chapter 7 is a vivid thread that recounts the journey of breaking free from the suffocating shackles of poverty. It's a chapter marked by dedication, persistence, and a refusal to be defined by circumstances. Here, I share the story of resilience in the face of adversity.

Short Story: Breaking Free from Shackles

Poverty had been a constant companion throughout my upbringing, casting a long shadow over my family's life. Its effects were pervasive, from the modest meals on our table to the threadbare clothes we wore. But I had learned from the elders that poverty need not be a life sentence; it could be defeated through education, hard work, and an unwavering determination to rise above it.

The journey to overcome poverty was far from easy. It demanded sacrifices and a commitment to breaking the cycle that had ensnared my family for generations. It meant pursuing education with fervour, seeking opportunities where others saw obstacles, and refusing to be defined by the circumstances of my birth.

Advice: Poverty Can Be Defeated

The elders had shared stories of their own battles with poverty, emphasizing that education and hard work were the most potent weapons in the fight. They spoke of how they had seized every opportunity to better their lives, even in the face of daunting odds. Their counsel was clear: poverty was a circumstance, not a destiny, and it could be defeated through resilience and unwavering resolve.

They taught me that the pursuit of knowledge was a powerful antidote to poverty. Education, they said, opened doors that were otherwise firmly shut. It was the key to unlocking opportunities and charting a path towards a better life.

Lesson: Poverty is a Circumstance, Not a Destiny

Through their guidance, I came to understand that poverty did not define who I was or what I could become. It was a circumstance that could be transcended through determination, hard work, and a refusal to give up. The lesson was clear: poverty was a chapter in my life, not the entire story.

This chapter stands as a testament to the indomitable human spirit's ability to triumph over adversity. It is a reminder that poverty, while a formidable adversary, can be conquered through education, resilience, and an unwavering commitment to a brighter future. In the pages that follow, I will delve deeper into how this mindset led me to break free from the grip of poverty and how it can inspire others to do the same.

The church elders had taught me that the path to overcoming poverty began with a commitment to education and personal growth.

One of the most significant lessons I learned was that poverty could be defeated through education. It was the key that unlocked doors to opportunities previously beyond reach. The elders' stories of their own journeys from humble beginnings to successful careers were living proof that education was a pathway to a brighter future.

Resilience played a pivotal role in breaking free from poverty's grip. It was the unwavering determination to persevere in the face of challenges and setbacks. The elders' narratives were filled with examples of resilience, showcasing their ability to bounce back from adversity with grace and determination.

The commitment to a brighter future was a driving force in my journey. It was the belief that poverty was not my destiny but merely a temporary state of affairs. This mindset fuelled my pursuit of knowledge and personal growth, as I understood that a better life was within reach if I was willing to work for it.

Breaking free from poverty also required financial literacy and prudent decision-making. The elders shared valuable lessons about managing finances, saving, and making wise investments. These insights empowered me to make informed choices about my financial future.

Community support was another essential element in overcoming poverty. The willingness of individuals to lend a helping hand, whether through mentorship, guidance, or opportunities, was instrumental in my journey. It reinforced the idea that we were not alone in our pursuit of a better life.

Reflection Question: How can a change in mindset help you overcome financial challenges?

Exercise: Develop a personal budget and savings plan to work toward financial stability.

CHAPTER 8

CHAPTER 8

Passing It On

Short Story: The joy of helping others escape the cycle of poverty

Passing It On

In the pages of my life, Chapter 8 is a reflection of the joy found in helping others escape the suffocating cycle of poverty. It's a chapter that embodies the belief that success is most meaningful when shared and used to uplift those still struggling in the shadows.

Short Story: The Joy of Helping Others

As I ascended the ladder of success, I realized that one of the most profound joys in life came from extending a hand to those who were still trapped in the cycle of poverty. It was a realization born from the teachings of the elders and a deep-rooted belief that success was not an isolated achievement but a platform from which to uplift others.

I witnessed the transformative power of education, hard work, and determination in my own life, and it became my mission to ensure that others could experience the same transformation. It was a journey of giving back, of using the resources and knowledge I had gained to create opportunities for those still facing the daunting spectre of poverty.

Advice: Use Your Success to Uplift Others

The elders had imparted a valuable lesson: that true success was not measured solely by personal accomplishments but by the impact one had on the lives of others. They shared stories of individuals who had used their success to uplift entire communities, leaving behind a legacy of positive change.

Their counsel was clear: the greatest legacy one could leave was not in material wealth or personal accolades, but in the lives transformed and the hope restored. They encouraged me to use my success as a tool for empowerment, to create opportunities where there were none, and to be a beacon of inspiration for those still navigating the shadows of poverty.

Lesson: Your Story Can Inspire Others

Through their guidance, I came to understand that my story had the power to inspire others to change their lives. It was a lesson in the ripple effect of inspiration, where one act of kindness and mentorship could set in motion a chain of positive transformation that extended far beyond what the eye could see.

This chapter stands as a testament to the belief that success is not an endpoint but a beginning, a platform from which to uplift others and create a brighter future. It is a reminder that the true measure of our achievements lies in the impact we have on the lives of those around us. In the pages that follow, I will share how this belief became a guiding principle in my life and how it can inspire others to make a difference in the world.

Using one's success to uplift others also meant being a mentor and a source of guidance. The church elders had served as mentors to me, and I, in turn, sought to mentor others, especially young people facing similar challenges. The cycle of mentorship was a powerful way to pass on knowledge and support the next generation.

Community engagement and giving back were integral components of this philosophy. The elders were actively involved in community projects and initiatives aimed at improving the well-being of others. Their example inspired me to seek opportunities to contribute to the betterment of my own community.

Reflection Question: In what ways can you use your success to uplift others?

Exercise: Identify one way you can give back to your community or support someone on their journey.

CHAPTER
9

Chapter 9

✣ *Inheritance of Love and Loss*

In the absence of my father, adversity loomed large over our family like a dark cloud, casting shadows of uncertainty and despair. Help was scarce, and in our moments of desperation, it was the unwavering love of my grandparents that offered a glimmer of hope amidst the storm.

As we grappled with the challenges of life without our father, my grandparents became beacons of light in the darkness, their love and support providing solace in our time of need. Despite their own struggles and limitations, they opened their hearts and homes to us, offering refuge from the harsh realities of the world. Every visit to their humble abode was met with warmth and affection, as they showered us with love and wisdom, imparting lessons that would shape our lives forever. Their talks of inheritance, though tinged with sadness, served as a reminder of their unwavering commitment to our well-being, even in their absence. But fate is a cruel mistress, and in the blink of an eye, tragedy struck once more. My grandmother, the pillar of strength in our family, fell ill with a mysterious ailment that left us all reeling with fear and uncertainty. Despite our efforts to find a cure, her condition only worsened, until one fateful morning, she slipped away from us, leaving behind a void that could never be filled. In the aftermath of her passing, my grandfather, burdened by grief and loneliness, succumbed to the weight of his sorrow, his health rapidly deteriorating until he too joined his beloved wife in the realm of the departed. With their passing, we were left with empty houses and heavy hearts, but also with a profound sense of gratitude for the love and support they had bestowed upon us. In the quiet solitude of their homes, we found solace and connection to our lost loved ones, their memories guiding us forward on our journey through life. And as we navigate the challenges that lie ahead, we carry with us the lessons of love, resilience, and gratitude that they so generously imparted.

Lessons Learned: The importance of family support during times of adversity. The fragility of life and the need to cherish every moment with loved ones. The resilience of the human spirit in the face of loss and grief.

Self-Reflective Questions: How has adversity shaped my perspective on life and family? What lessons have I learned from the experiences of loss and grief? How can I honour the memory of my grandparents and carry their legacy forward?

Gratitude Motivation: In the face of adversity, it is often the love and support of family that sustains us. Let us express gratitude for the moments of joy and the lessons learned from the challenges we face, and let us carry forward the legacy of love and resilience that our grandparents have bestowed upon us.

CHAPTER 10

Chapter 10

Failure Is Not an Option

Short Story: The realization that failure is not an option when you're determined to succeed.

Failure Is Not an Option

Within the chapters of my life, Chapter 9 stands as a testament to the unwavering belief that failure is not an option when one is determined to succeed. It's a chapter that underscores the resilience required to navigate the unpredictable waters of life and to never allow setbacks to extinguish the flames of determination.

Short Story: The Realization

The realization that failure is not an option became a defining moment in my journey. It was a lesson born from countless trials and tribulations, from moments when success seemed distant and the weight of adversity threatened to crush my spirit. Yet, I refused to surrender to the possibility of failure.

I had learned from the elders that adversity and setbacks were not signs of weakness but opportunities for growth. They shared stories of their own failures and the resilience it had taken to rise above them. It was a realization that failure, far from being an endpoint, was often a stepping stone to success.

Advice: Never Be Afraid of Failure

The elders had instilled in me the courage to face failure head-on, to view it not as a mark of defeat but as a challenge to overcome. They taught me that those who never tasted failure often never truly tasted success either. Failure was the crucible in which character was forged and determination tested.

Their counsel was clear: never be afraid of failure, for it is through failure that we learn, grow, and evolve. It is a necessary companion on the path to success, a teacher whose lessons are invaluable.

Lesson: Success is Worth the Effort

Through their guidance, I came to understand that, while success was not guaranteed, the pursuit of it was worth every effort. It was a lesson in resilience, in the indomitable spirit that refuses to be deterred by setbacks or obstacles. Success, they taught me, was not a destination but a journey, and the journey itself was a reward.

This chapter serves as a reminder that the pursuit of success is a testament to the human spirit's resilience and determination. It is a declaration that failure is not an option when fuelled by unwavering belief and the courage to persevere. In the pages that follow, I will share how this mindset propelled me forward on my journey and how it can inspire others to overcome obstacles and pursue their own dreams with unwavering determination.

The belief that failure is not an option was a mantra that echoed in my mind throughout my journey. It was a conviction that propelled me forward, even in the face of daunting challenges. This mindset taught me that setbacks were not roadblocks but stepping stones on the path to success.

One of the most profound lessons I learned was that failure, far from being a final destination, was often a necessary part of the journey. The church elders shared stories of their own failures and how they had used them as opportunities for growth and learning. This perspective shifted my perception of failure from one of fear to one of resilience.

The courage to persevere in the face of adversity was a hallmark of this mindset. It meant not allowing setbacks or obstacles to deter me from my goals. It required a deep inner resolve to keep moving forward, even when the path seemed uncertain.

I also learned that unwavering belief in oneself was a powerful force. The elders taught me that self-doubt could be one of the greatest obstacles to success. Belief in oneself, coupled with a determination to overcome challenges, could move mountains.

This mindset of "failure is not an option" was not about denying the existence of obstacles or difficulties. It was about confronting them head-on with courage and tenacity. It was a declaration that, no matter how steep the climb, I would not give up on my dreams.

As I reflect on this chapter of my life, I am reminded that the pursuit of success is a testament to the resilience and determination of the human spirit. It is a declaration that failure is not an option when fuelled by unwavering belief and the courage to persevere. This mindset has the power to propel individuals forward on their journeys, enabling them to overcome obstacles and pursue their dreams with unwavering determination.

Reflection Question: How has your perspective on failure evolved as you've pursued your goals?

Exercise: Write a "failure manifesto" that reminds you why failure is a stepping stone to success.

CHAPTER 11

Chapter 11

✤ *The Legacy of Resilience*

Short Story: A reflection on the journey from a fatherless childhood to a life filled with purpose.
: The Legacy of Resilience

Short Story: As I sit here, reflecting on the tumultuous journey from a fatherless childhood to a life filled with purpose, I can't help but marvel at the twists and turns life has presented. The story of the boychild without a father is not unique, but it's one of enduring hope. It's a narrative that demonstrates that ourcircumstances, no matter how dire, do not determine our destiny.

Advice: Life doesn't always hand us a fair deck of cards. We might start with less, face more obstacles, or find ourselves without a roadmap. But remember, it's not where you start those matters; it's where you finish. Embrace the mentors and role models who enter your life, for they hold the keys to knowledge and guidance that can alter your course. A strong support system is invaluable.

Lesson: Your past does not define you; it refines you. Every hardship, every challenge, and every adversity you encounter has the potential to mold you into a person of strength, resilience, and character. It's not the absence of difficulties that shapes us but rather how we respond to them. When life pushes you down, summon the will to rise again, for your destiny is not determined by the hand you're dealt but by how you choose to play it.

Reflection Question: How can a healthy self-concept enhance your ability to love and be loved?

Exercise: Create a list of qualities you admire in yourself and qualities you aspire to develop.

Reflection Question: What self-love practices can you incorporate into your daily life to nurture a healthy self-concept?

Exercise: Start a gratitude journal, noting three things you appreciate about yourself every day.

CHAPTER 12

CHAPTER 12

The Uncharted Path

The Boychild That Could Have Been

The story of a boychild without a father could have been a tragic tale, one marked by despair, hardship, and endless obstacles. Growing up in the absence of paternal guidance, my early years were fraught with uncertainty. It's not hard to imagine the trajectory my life could have taken had I not chosen a different path.

Challenges loomed large at every corner. The absence of a father figure meant that I had to navigate the intricate maze of life alone. The lack of proper education, a shadow that cast itself upon many aspects of my youth, could have forever limited my potential. But in every challenge, there is an opportunity, and my journey was about seizing those opportunities.

The Steps Toward Self-Improvement

The Quest for Knowledge: One of the earliest decisions I made was to become a lifelong learner. I understood that education could be my ticket to a better life. So, I devoured books, sought out mentors, and attended workshops. Every scrap of knowledge was like a stepping stone on my path to self-improvement.

Building Resilience: Challenges are inevitable, and my life was not devoid of them. Instead of succumbing to adversity, I embraced it. With each setback, I became more resilient. It wasn't about avoiding failure; it was about bouncing back stronger.

The Birth of a Business: As I accumulated knowledge and experience, I realized that I had a passion for automotive preservation technology. With the courage to take the plunge, I started my first business. It was small and modest, but it was a dream brought to life.

Venturing into the Marketing World: My journey wasn't confined to a single field. I had a deep curiosity about marketing, and I decided to venture into this dynamic and ever-evolving world. Breaking sales records became a common theme, and I realized that success is not about what you sell but how you sell it.

The Birth of a Training Company: Armed with the expertise I'd gathered over the years, I ventured into a new territory: education. I started my own training company, not only to impart knowledge but also to inspire others to rise above their circumstances.

The Automotive Preservation Technology Business

I remember the day I opened my first automotive preservation technology business vividly. It was a small mobile, but it represented more than just a place of work. It symbolized the culmination of years of hard work, determination, and a refusal to accept failure as my inheritance.

In this business, I honed my technical skills. I was not just an entrepreneur; I became an expert in my field. Each car that passed through my workshop was a testament to my dedication to the craft.

Venturing into the Marketing World

The transition into the marketing world was both exhilarating and challenging. I was no longer tinkering with engines but with consumer psychology. It was a world of strategy, creativity, and relentless adaptation.

Breaking sales records became a common occurrence, not because I had some secret formula, but because I understood the power of connecting with people. I learned that sales are not about pushing products; they are about solving problems and fulfilling needs.

The Birth of a Training Company

As my journey continued, I realized that my true calling was not just in business but in education. I founded my own training company, aiming to empower others with the knowledge and skills they needed to overcome their own challenges. It was a full-circle moment, as I, the boychild without a father, became a mentor and guide to others.

CHAPTER 13

Chapter 13

"From Sales Apprentice to Entrepreneurial Visionary"

As I embarked on my journey into the world of sales and marketing, I was fuelled by a burning desire to learn and grow, to transcend the limitations of my circumstances, and to create a better future for myself and my family. While some saw only the challenges inherent in commission-based structures, I saw an opportunity to harness my skills and determination to achieve financial freedom and security.

With every challenge I encountered, I saw an opportunity to learn and grow, to refine my craft, and to master the art of salesmanship. I immersed myself in the intricacies of the industry, soaking up knowledge like a sponge and honing my skills with each passing day. But beyond just mastering the art of selling, I realised that true success lay in leadership and entrepreneurship.

Armed with the knowledge and skills I had acquired, I set my sights on a loftier goal: starting my own business. I envisioned a company that would not only provide for my family but also make a positive impact on the world around me. And thus, Link to Emerge International was born—a venture that combined my passion for automobiles with a commitment to providing clean water solutions to communities in need.

But starting a business was no easy feat. It required dedication, resilience, and a willingness to embrace uncertainty. I took on multiple roles within the company, from sales and administration to finance and operations, wearing many hats as I navigated the challenges of entrepreneurship.

Despite the obstacles I faced, I remained steadfast in my vision, tirelessly working to build Link to Emerge International into a thriving enterprise. I leveraged my skills in sales and marketing to expand our reach, from humble beginnings selling services on the streets to establishing a fully operational workshop.

Through perseverance and determination, I not only achieved my entrepreneurial dreams but also empowered others to do the same. I trained and mentored individuals to join me on this journey, sharing my knowledge and expertise to help them unlock their full potential.

Guidelines for Entrepreneurial Success:

- Identify your strengths and passions, and leverage them to create opportunities.
- Continuously invest in learning and skill development to stay ahead in your industry.
- Embrace challenges as opportunities for growth and innovation.
- Surround yourself with a supportive network of mentors and peers who can offer guidance and encouragement.
- Stay focused on your vision, and never lose sight of the impact you want to make in the world.
-

Empowerment through Entrepreneurship:

By harnessing your skills and talents, you have the power to create something truly remarkable. Don't be afraid to take risks, embrace failure as a learning opportunity, and never underestimate the impact you can have as an entrepreneur. With determination and perseverance, anything is possible.

CHAPTER 14

Chapter 14

✤ *In the Hallowed Halls of My School*

"In the hallowed halls of Esau Mosedame Primary School, nestled amidst the bustling streets of our neighbourhood, a seed of inspiration was planted, destined to take root and flourish in the fertile soil of young hearts and impressionable minds."

It was in the innocence of my sixth grade year that fate intertwined with destiny, casting me into a pivotal role in shaping the narrative of hope and resilience that would come to define my journey. Little did I know that a simple conversation with our computer tutor, affectionately known as Comrade, would sow the seeds of a powerful message that would reverberate far beyond the confines of our classroom walls.

As Comrade embarked on the noble task of crafting a speech to uplift and empower our fellow learners, he turned to me, a quiet yet observant student, for insight into my personal experiences. With gentle curiosity, he delved into the recesses of my heart, seeking to understand the challenges and triumphs that shaped my young life.

In that moment, as I shared snippets of my journey with Comrade, a spark ignited within me, illuminating the path forward with newfound clarity and purpose. It was as though the words flowed effortlessly from my lips, each syllable infused with the resilience and determination that had carried me through life's trials and tribulations.

As Comrade meticulously wove my words into the fabric of his speech, a title emerged that encapsulated the essence of our shared journey: "Failure is not my inheritance." It was a declaration of defiance against the odds, a testament to the power of hope and perseverance in the face of adversity.

Little did I realise the profound impact that those words would have, not only on my fellow learners but on the countless souls who would encounter them in the years to come. They became a rallying cry for those who dared to dream beyond their circumstances, a beacon of light in the darkest of nights.

And so, in the humble confines of our primary school classroom, a seed of inspiration was planted, its roots stretching deep into the fertile soil of young hearts and impressionable minds, forever changing the trajectory of our lives.

CHAPTER 15

Chapter 15

✢ *The Legacy of a Boychild's Journey*

As I reflect on my journey from a fatherless boychild to a responsible, empowered adult, I can't help but marvel at the twists and turns life has presented. It's proof that our circumstances do not define us; they refine us. My story is a testament to the transformative power of education, mentorship, responsibility, and hard work.

In the chapters that follow, I'll delve deeper into the lessons learned and the wisdom gained throughout my journey. From the depths of adversity to the pinnacle of achievement, my story is a testament to the indomitable human spirit and the belief that failure is not our inheritance; it's a challenge to overcome. May this story inspire you to embark on your own path of transformation and fulfilment, for your journey is a story waiting to be written, and I am living proof that the human spirit is capable of remarkable feats.

CHAPTER 16

Chapter 16

The Guiding Hand of Faith

The Role of Faith in My Life

Faith, an unwavering belief in something greater than ourselves, has been the cornerstone of my journey from a fatherless boychild to an independent individual. From my earliest memories, I was introduced to the world of faith through the church. It was in those hallowed halls that I discovered not only the power of spirituality but also the incredible strength it could provide in the face of adversity.

My strong Christian belief system was more than just a set of rituals; it was a guiding force. It was a belief that there was a divine plan for my life and that no matter the challenges I faced, I was not alone. This belief was a comforting presence, a source of hope when times were tough, and a wellspring of courage when I needed to take risks.

The Church as a Second Home

For a boychild without a father, the church became more than just a place of worship; it was a second home. It was where I found mentors who stepped into the role of a guiding father figure. These wise individuals provided not only spiritual guidance but also life lessons that shaped my character. They taught me the importance of humility, kindness, and the power of forgiveness.

In moments of doubt and despair, it was my faith that carried me forward. The belief that there was a higher purpose to my life allowed me to endure challenges with resilience and grace. It was through prayer and introspection that I found the strength to persevere, to believe in myself, and to keep moving forward, even when the odds seemed insurmountable.

A Moral Compass in a Chaotic World

As I navigated the complexities of life, my faith served as a moral compass. It was a steadfast reminder of the values and principles that should guide my actions. In a world that often seemed chaotic and morally ambiguous, my Christian beliefs provided clarity and direction. They reminded me that success was not measured solely in material wealth but in the impact I had on others and the integrity of my character.

My journey was not without its share of setbacks and disappointments. But even in those moments, I held fast to my faith, believing that adversity was not a punishment but a test of my strength. It was through these trials that I grew stronger, more resilient, and more determined to fulfil the purpose I believed God had set before me.

CHAPTER 17

Chapter 17

A Life of Independence

The Intersection of Faith and Independence

My faith in God played a profound role in my path toward independence. It was not a faith that passively waited for divine intervention but one that encouraged action and responsibility. I believed that God had equipped me with the talents and abilities needed to overcome challenges and make a positive impact on the world.

With this belief in mind, I ventured into the world of entrepreneurship. My strong Christian faith was not a hindrance but a driving force. It pushed me to be ethical, to treat others with respect, and to approach business with honesty and integrity. In every business endeavour, I sought to reflect the values instilled in me through my faith.

Inspiring Others Through Faith

As I achieved success in the business world, I realized that my journey could inspire others. It wasn't just about personal achievement but about showing that faith could be a guiding light in the darkest of times. I wanted to share my story, not as a testament to my abilities but as a testament to the transformative power of faith.

Through speaking engagements, mentoring, and outreach, I began to inspire others to believe in themselves and to have faith in their own journeys. I emphasized that faith was not a passive belief but an active force that could drive change and transformation. My story served as evidence that a strong belief system could be the catalyst for personal growth and independence.

CHAPTER 18

Chapter 18

Leaving a Legacy of Faith

The Legacy I Hope to Leave

As I look back on my journey from a fatherless boychild to an independent individual, I hope that my legacy will be one of faith. A legacy that shows the world that no matter the challenges we face, faith can be a guiding light. It can empower us to overcome adversity, make a positive impact on others, and achieve our dreams.

I hope that my story inspires others to embrace their faith, to believe in themselves, and to pursue their own paths of independence. It's not about the absence of challenges; it's about having the faith to overcome them. It's about recognizing that failure is not our inheritance; it's a test of our faith and determination.

In closing, I believe that faith is not just a personal belief; it's a force for good in the world. It can lead us to a life of purpose, independence, and fulfilment. My journey is a testament to the power of faith, and I hope that it encourages others to embark on their own journeys with unwavering belief in the possibilities that lie.

CHAPTER 19

Chapter 19

The Heart of the Journey: A Mother's Love

A Single Mother's Sacrifice

At the very core of my journey, the beacon that illuminated the path from a fatherless boychild to a person of independence was the unwavering love and sacrifice of my single mother. She was not only the guiding star in my life but also the embodiment of faith and resilience. Her story is one of profound dedication and selflessness, a testament to the incredible power of a mother's love.

Through the darkest of days, my mother stood as a pillar of strength. Her love knew no bounds, and her sacrifices were immeasurable. She deprived herself of personal desires, luxuries, and comforts to ensure that her children had the opportunities she wished for them. Her unwavering faith in God served as the foundation upon which she built our family, providing us with a moral compass to navigate the challenges that life presented.

A Mother's Role in Fostering Faith

As I reflect on my journey, I realize that it was my mother who instilled the seed of faith in my heart. Her prayers and guidance were instrumental in shaping my belief system. She taught me that faith was not just a set of beliefs but a way of life, a compass that could guide us through life's storms.

It was my mother who encouraged me to trust in God's plan, even when the path seemed uncertain. She showed me that faith was not a shield against adversity but a source of strength to endure it. Through her example, she demonstrated that a single parent, armed with faith and love, could raise children who were not defined by their circumstances but empowered to transcend them.

Empowering Single Parents Through Faith

To all the single parents who may be reading my story, I want to emphasize the importance of faith and love in raising children. Your role is not defined by the absence of a partner; it is defined by your ability to provide love, support, and guidance. Just as my mother empowered me, you have the power to empower your children.

Encourage them to have faith in themselves and in the divine plan that guides their lives. Teach them that adversity is not a roadblock but a stepping stone to growth and resilience. Show them that love and sacrifice are the greatest gifts a parent can give and that they have the strength within them to overcome any challenge.

CHAPTER 20

Chapter 20

✚ *A Legacy of Love and Faith*

As I near the end of my story, I hope that my journey serves as a testament to the incredible impact that a single parent's love and faith can have on a child's life. My mother's sacrifice and unwavering support laid the foundation for my independence and success. Her faith was not only a guiding light but also a source of inspiration.

To single parents, I say this: Your journey may be filled with challenges, but it is also filled with opportunities to inspire and empower your children. Your love and faith can shape their character, instil resilience, and equip them to face the world with confidence. Remember that you are not alone; you have the power to be the guiding star in your child's life, leading them to a future filled with promise and purpose.

In closing, my story is not just one of faith and independence; it is a tribute to the love and sacrifice of a single mother who believed in the power of faith to transcend circumstances. May my journey inspire you to raise your children in faith and love, nurturing their belief in themselves and in the extraordinary possibilities that lie ahead.

CHAPTER 21

Chapter 21

Brotherhood and Redemption

The Complex Bond with My Brother

In the intricate tapestry of my journey, the thread of brotherhood weaves a compelling narrative. My relationship with my older brother was marked by both strife and redemption, a testament to the profound impact our father's absence had on each of us. While my mother's love and faith were guiding stars in my life, my brother's journey was a different one, shaped by anger, confusion, and the belief that being a man meant wielding power.

Our father's death cast a long shadow over our childhood. For my brother, it was a weight too heavy to bear. Anger became his armour, and defiance became his shield. He believed that to be a man was to be heard, even if it meant using power and aggression. Our relationship was marked by arguments and fights, each of us struggling to find our place in a world without our father's guidance.

The Path of Redemption

Despite the turmoil of our early years, I was determined to find a better way, not just for myself but for my brother as well. I understood that anger and aggression were not the path to manhood but a detour away from it. It was through my faith and the lessons imparted by our church elders that I began to seek a different path.

I became a sponge for wisdom, absorbing every piece of advice and guidance offered by those older and wiser than me. I knew that if I wanted to become a responsible man, I needed to learn from those who had walked the path before me. It meant depriving myself of the opportunities to play with other kids fully, but it was a sacrifice I was willing to make.

The Transformation of a Boychild

As I embarked on my journey of transformation, I made it a mission to extend a helping hand to my brother. I realized that he, too, was a victim of our circumstances and that anger was a manifestation of his pain. Slowly but surely, I began to share the wisdom I had gathered from the church elders and my own experiences.

It was not an easy process, but over time, my brother began to change. He saw in my actions and choices a different way of being a man, one that did not rely on aggression but on wisdom, empathy, and strength of character. Our relationship transformed from one of conflict to one of mutual respect and support.

CHAPTER 22

Chapter 22

The Journey of Two Brothers

Brotherhood Redefined

Our journey as brothers was not without its struggles, but it was also a testament to the power of transformation and redemption. As we both learned and grew, we redefined what it meant to be men. It was not about dominance or aggression; it was about responsibility and leadership, tempered by empathy and wisdom.

My brother's anger, once a raging fire, became a controlled flame that fuelled his determination to make a positive impact. He learned to listen, to seek guidance, and to channel his energy into productive endeavours. Together, we discovered that true strength lay not in the ability to overpower others but in the capacity to uplift and inspire.

CHAPTER 23

Chapter 23

 *Lessons Learnt*

The Wisdom of Elders

In the chapters that follow, I will delve deeper into the lessons learned and the wisdom gained on this remarkable journey. From the complexities of brotherhood to the transformative power of faith, my story is a testament to the indomitable human spirit and the belief that we have the capacity to rise above our circumstances.

For single parents, I hope my journey serves as a reminder that love, faith, and guidance can shape the character of your children and empower them to transcend their challenges. To brothers who may be struggling, I offer the example of our transformation as proof that anger and aggression need not define manhood. There is a better way, one marked by wisdom, empathy, and responsibility.

In closing, the journey of two brothers, one marked by strife and the other by transformation, is a story of redemption and hope. It demonstrates that even in the face of adversity and anger, there is the potential for growth, change, and the discovery of a more enlightened path to becoming responsible men.

CHAPTER 24

Chapter 24

Triumph Over Adversity: The Power of Unity

The Desperate Days

In the pages preceding this one, I've shared a narrative of struggle, transformation, and redemption. It's a journey that began in the absence of a father, with limited financial means, and days when putting food on the table was a formidable challenge. These are the circumstances that far too many families find themselves in, where hope seems like a distant dream and the world appears to look down upon you.

In our community, the prevailing sentiment was often one of pity or judgment. People wondered how a single parent, uneducated and struggling financially, could provide a future for her children. Yet, it was precisely during these trying times that the power of unity and the love of God emerged as our guiding forces.

The Power of Unity

As a family, we recognized that our only way forward was through unity. We became a tightly knit team, supporting and uplifting each other through the darkest of days. My mother, despite her limited education, instilled in us the values of hard work, determination, and faith. These were our tools for survival, and we wielded them with unwavering resolve.

In the face of adversity, we pooled our resources, both tangible and intangible. We shared the little we had, understanding that together we were stronger. My older brother's determination to find a job in the mines became a beacon of hope, while my sister's commitment to her studies and her eventual successful marriage symbolized the triumph of resilience over circumstance.

The Power of Grace

In our journey, grace was a recurring theme. It was the inexplicable moments of help and support from unexpected sources, the doors that opened when we needed them most, and the blessings that seemed to arrive just in time. We recognized that grace was not a random occurrence but a manifestation of the love of God working through the disadvantaged.

As I became the first graduate in our family and ventured into the world of running businesses, I couldn't help but see the hand of grace guiding my steps. It was as if the universe conspired to propel us forward, despite our humble beginnings. We knew that we were recipients of a divine grace that defied the odds and allowed us to break the cycle of disadvantage.

CHAPTER 25

Chapter 25

A Testament to God's Love

Transformed Lives

Today, as I look at my family and the journey we've undertaken, I see transformed lives. From a single parent struggling to make ends meet, we've evolved into a family where dreams have been realized. I've gone on to run successful companies; my brother found employment in the mines; my sister built a successful marriage; and my little sister completed her high school studies.

Our story is not just about our personal achievements but a testament to what God can do for the disadvantaged. It's a story of grace, unity, and the power of love to overcome adversity. We stand as living proof that the circumstances you're born into need not determine your destiny. With faith, determination, and the support of loved ones, you can overcome even the most daunting challenges.

A Message of Hope

To those who find themselves in similar circumstances, I offer a message of hope. Know that adversity is not the end of your story; it's just a chapter. The power of unity, the love of God, and the grace that flows even in the darkest moments can carry you through to a brighter future.

In our journey, we learned that when a family stands together and supports each other through thick and thin, incredible transformations can occur. Adversity may shape your story, but it doesn't define your future. Through faith, unity, and the love of God, you too can overcome the odds and create a legacy of triumph over adversity.

CHAPTER 26

Chapter 26

✤ *"Divine Intervention: A Taste of Grace"*

In the hustle and bustle of Johannesburg, where dreams often collided with reality, I found myself at a crossroads—both figuratively and literally. It was a moment that would reaffirm my faith in the divine and the presence of angels in our midst.

As fate would have it, I had journeyed from my hometown of Polokwane to the bustling city of Johannesburg with a fellow trainee. Our paths had aligned, and we were now colleagues, with him being my superior as the training manager. Little did I know that this journey would take an unexpected turn, one that would test not only my resilience but also my belief in the grace of God.

The stage was set for our end-of-year production, a critical moment in our careers. But as the days drew nearer, an unsettling cloud began to form. My once-trusted colleague turned against me, swaying the entire team to his side in a bid to diminish my chances of topping the awards.

As if that wasn't enough, a strange ailment suddenly struck me. My joints weakened, leaving me almost paralyzed, and my energy dwindled to a mere flicker. I was famished, and my pocket held nothing but a solitary R2 coin. It was a dire situation.

In the depths of my despair, a thought—perhaps a divine whisper—urged me to find solace in a simple meal: pap and fish. The problem? I didn't have the R20 needed to purchase it. Desperate and depleted, I reached out to family for assistance.

My aunt, my lifeline at that moment, sent R50 during her lunch break through a Shoprite money transfer. But fate, with its peculiar sense of humour, had other plans. Instead of providing me with the necessary ten-digit reference number, she inadvertently sent eleven.

I was left stranded, my aunt's phone unreachable, and my hopes hanging by the thinnest thread. I feared that I might end up in the hospital or worse.

In my darkest hour, when despair threatened to consume me, something extraordinary happened. An elderly woman, dressed entirely in blue and radiating an aura of kindness, approached me. Her presence was calming, and she addressed me in our native tongue rather than the predominant Zulu.

She reached into her purse and withdrew a humble R20 note. With a soft, reassuring voice, she said, "My son, take this money and buy yourself the food you came here for."

I stood there, awestruck and deeply moved. I stammered in astonishment, "Huh?" She raised her voice slightly, repeating her words, but it was as if she didn't want to draw attention.

I hurriedly grabbed a plate of pap and fish, my hands trembling with gratitude and disbelief. But when I turned around to thank her, she had vanished into thin air. None of my colleagues saw her, and inquiries led to baffled expressions. It was as if she had appeared solely for me.

The moment I began eating that meal, I felt a surge of strength coursing through my veins. It was a miraculous transformation. With newfound vigour, I returned to work, determined to give it my all.

The odds were stacked against me, with everyone in the office seemingly ahead in sales. But when the final day arrived, I defied all expectations and clinched the coveted award for Best Sales Training Manager—not once but twice.

As I stood on that stage, clutching my well-deserved awards, I knew in my heart that I had witnessed the grace of God. It was a moment that underscored the presence of benevolent forces in our lives, ready to step in when we need them the most.

That incident remains etched in my memory as a testament to the miraculous, the unexplained, and the profound belief that divine intervention can manifest in the most unexpected ways. In those challenging times, I had not only discovered the grace of God but also encountered an angel in disguise, reminding me that in the midst of darkness, a glimmer of hope can shine through.

My journey, fraught with adversity, had been touched by grace, and it was a story I would carry with me as an everlasting testament to the existence of a higher power and the kindness that dwells among us. It was a story of grace, belief, and the unwavering conviction that miracles are real.

CHAPTER 27

Chapter 27

✣ *"A Test of Faith: Surrendering to the Divine"*

In the journey of life, there are moments that test not only our resolve but the very core of our faith. These are the moments when we find ourselves at the crossroads of despair and hope, where the choices we make can shape our destiny in unforeseen ways.

One fateful night, the clock had struck a late 21h00, and the office was closing its doors. I found myself in the company of colleagues, a camaraderie that was about to be tested in a way I could never have imagined. Little did I know that this night would become a poignant chapter in my story of faith, a chapter that would ultimately reaffirm my unwavering belief in the divine.

As we bid farewell to the office, I did not realize that I had forgotten to withdraw money for my transport home. It was a critical oversight, one that would lead to a predicament I couldn't have foreseen. The banks had closed their doors, and the shops had turned off their lights, leaving me stranded in the heart of the city with no means to get back home.

In my moment of desperation, I turned to my colleagues, hoping that they would extend a helping hand in my time of need. I mustered the courage to ask for a transport fare, a small loan that I could repay the following morning. To my disbelief, they refused and left me behind, their departing footsteps echoing through the empty streets.

Alone and disheartened, I walked to the taxi rank, hoping to find a taxi that could take me at least part of the way home. But as fate would have it, only two taxis remained, the last lifelines of the night. I approached the drivers with a plea, my voice carrying the weight of desperation. I explained my situation and my promise to repay them in the near future, but they were locked in a heated argument, oblivious to my plight.

In that solitary moment, a profound sense of hopelessness washed over me. The thought of spending the night on the unforgiving streets of the city, in my office attire no less, filled me with a bone-chilling dread. It was a situation that tested not only my patience but also the very essence of my faith.

In that moment of surrender, when I had no other recourse but to relinquish control, I turned my gaze heavenward. I entrusted my predicament to a higher power, surrendering to the uncertainty of the night. I let go of the need to control my circumstances and placed my faith in the divine, a humble acknowledgment that I was not alone in my struggle.

And then, as if in response to my unspoken plea, a miracle unfolded. My boss, who had long departed from the office hours earlier, appeared before me in his car. It was a sight I could never have anticipated, for I had believed he was miles away from that place.

As the traffic light turned red and his vehicle came to a halt, I ran towards his car, my heart pounding with a mix of relief and gratitude. He peered out of the window, his face initially etched with shock, as if he believed he was being accosted. But as soon as he recognized me, he swiftly unlocked the door and let me in.

The drive home was an unusual one, marked by an unspoken understanding of the gravity of the moment. We shared a few words, for sometimes the most profound moments are shrouded in silence. I cried tears of gratitude and relief, my heart swelling with a profound sense of faith.

In that night's test of faith, I learned a powerful lesson: that surrendering to the divine and accepting our circumstances can lead to unexpected blessings. When we are at our lowest, when we relinquish control and place our trust in a higher power, that is often when the divine steps in to guide our way.

This chapter serves as a testament to the significance of faith, the importance of surrender, and the remarkable ways in which God comes through when we least expect it. It is a reminder that even in our darkest moments, there is a glimmer of hope, a guiding light that leads us home.

CHAPTER 28

Chapter 28

✣ *The Shadow of Absentee Parenting*

The Impact of Parental Absence on Relationships

Growing up without the love and guidance of both parents, I carried a burden that weighed on my relationships throughout my journey. The absence of a father figure left a void, not only in my own understanding of what it meant to be a man but also in my ability to navigate the complexities of romantic relationships. This absence created a fear of loving too much, a hesitation born from the fear of abandonment.

During the stages of puberty and the teenage years, when guidance and education on relationships are crucial, I found myself lacking the necessary tools. I often stumbled through the intricate dance of romance, making mistakes and hurting those I cared about. The absence of comprehensive education in these vital areas left me vulnerable to misunderstandings and missteps.

The Healing Power of Elders and Leaders

It was in the wisdom of elders and leaders that I found the balm for these wounds. Their guidance was instrumental in reshaping my perspective on love and relationships. They taught me that love should not be feared but embraced, and that vulnerability is not a weakness but a strength.

Through their counsel and mentorship, I learned to appreciate the value of open communication, empathy, and patience in building lasting relationships. It was through their wisdom that I began to heal from the scars of parental absence and the fear of abandonment.

In the chapters ahead, I'll delve deeper into the transformative impact of these mentors and how their guidance reshaped my approach to relationships. Their wisdom, born from a wealth of life experiences, became a guiding light in my journey toward healthier, more fulfilling connections with others.

CHAPTER 29

Chapter 29

The Journey into Fatherhood

The Uncertain Path of Fatherhood

Stepping into the role of a father was a transformative moment in my journey, yet it was a path I initially found fraught with uncertainty and challenges. As a young man, I lacked the guidance and preparation needed to navigate the complexities of parenthood. At first, I stumbled, unsure of how to be the father I wished to become.

It was my daughter, Rorisang, who became the turning point in my journey as a father. Her arrival was not just a new chapter; it was a driving force propelling me towards success. She became the reason why I had to work hard, provide the life I never had, and be the best father I could possibly be.

A Commitment to Fatherhood

Even after a difficult breakup with her mother, I made a commitment to be a present and supportive father. I refused to run away from responsibility, understanding that being a father meant more than just providing financially. It meant being emotionally present, offering guidance, and fostering a loving and supportive environment.

To young men like me, who may have lacked the ideal father figure growing up, I offer this advice: It's never too late to become the best father you can be. Parenthood is a journey of growth and learning, and even in the absence of a blueprint, your love, commitment, and dedication can shape the future of your children in profound ways. Embrace the opportunity to be a positive influence in their lives, for it is through your actions and presence that you can redefine the path of fatherhood for generations to come.

CHAPTER 30

Chapter 30

✥ *Navigating the Challenges of Fatherhood*

The Struggles of a Young Father

Becoming a father at a relatively young age was undeniably challenging. I found myself grappling with the responsibilities of parenthood while still in the process of shaping my own life. There were sleepless nights, diaper changes, and a constant sense of uncertainty about whether I was doing things right. The lack of a paternal figure in my own upbringing meant that I was essentially learning on the job, and it was far from easy.

The Driving Force: Rorisang

The moment I held Rorisang in my arms for the first time, something profound shifted within me. She became not just my daughter but also my reason for being. I was determined to provide her with opportunities and a loving environment that I hadn't experienced in my own childhood. Her laughter, her innocence, and her unwavering trust in me became the driving forces behind every decision I made.

I knew that if I wanted to be the best father to her, I had to work relentlessly to overcome the challenges before me. Rorisang's presence in my life was a constant reminder that I couldn't afford to falter. I had to be a role model, a source of strength, and a pillar of support for her.

Learning from past mistakes

A painful breakup with her mother served as a pivotal moment in my journey as a father. It was a period of self-reflection and realization. I understood that running away from responsibility was not an option.

Instead, I had to learn to be present, to communicate effectively, and to co-parent in the best interests of our daughter.

This transformation wasn't without its difficulties. It required humility, patience, and a willingness to put aside personal differences for the sake of our child. But in doing so, I discovered that being a father was not just about biology; it was about the choices I made and the actions I took.

Becoming the best father

To young men who may find themselves in similar circumstances, I offer this advice: Embrace the opportunity to be the best father you can be, regardless of how you were raised or the challenges you face. Parenthood is a journey filled with ups and downs, but it's also an incredible opportunity for personal growth and positive influence.

Learn from your past mistakes, seek guidance from mentors or support networks, and prioritize being present in your child's life. Understand that fatherhood is not defined by age but by the love, commitment, and dedication you bring to the role. Your actions today can shape the future of your child, and by embracing the responsibilities of fatherhood, you have the power to redefine the path of parenthood for generations to come.

CHAPTER 31

Chapter 31

Guiding Teenagers Through the Reckless Years

The Reckless Years of Teenagers

In today's fast-paced and complex world, the teenage years often bring forth a whirlwind of emotions, choices, and challenges. It's a time when the desire for independence clashes with the need for guidance, and the allure of risky behaviours can be particularly enticing. As someone who has navigated the treacherous waters of youth, I understand the allure of recklessness all too well.

Teenagers today face unique pressures that were not as prevalent in previous generations. The influence of social media, peer pressure, and the relentless pursuit of instant gratification can steer them down paths filled with poor decisions, from substance abuse to reckless relationships.

The Role of Guidance and Education

The key to guiding teenagers through these reckless years lies in providing them with the right guidance and education. It's crucial for parents, mentors, and educators to establish open lines of communication with teenagers, creating spaces where they feel safe to share their thoughts, fears, and uncertainties.

Teenagers need to understand the consequences of their actions, both in the short and long term. Education on topics such as substance abuse, safe relationships, and mental health should be readily available. It's not about sheltering them from the world but empowering them with knowledge and critical thinking skills to make informed choices.

Fostering Responsibility and Empathy

Encouraging responsibility is another key component of guiding teenagers through the reckless years. They should be taught the value of personal accountability for their actions, as well as the importance of empathy towards others. When they understand how their choices can affect not only their own lives but also the lives of those around them, it can serve as a powerful motivator for responsible behaviour.

Moreover, it's essential to lead by example. Teenagers often learn more from observing the behaviour of adults in their lives than from being told what to do. Demonstrating responsible and empathetic actions in your own life can have a profound impact on the values they adopt.

Navigating Different Upbringings: Rural vs. Suburban Boyhood

In this chapter, we delve into the stark differences in upbringing and experiences between the rural and suburban boychild. These disparities in environment, opportunities, and influences shape their views, behaviours, and ultimately, their paths in life. We also explore the solutions to empower both rural and suburban boychildren to make choices that lead to purposeful lives.

The Rural Boychild: Adversity and Resilience

Growing up in rural areas often means facing adversity at a young age. These boychildren may encounter limited access to education, healthcare, and economic opportunities. They are raised in close-knit communities where traditional values and a strong sense of community are prevalent. However, the absence of certain resources can hinder their personal growth and exposure to modernity.

Views and Behaviours of the Rural Boychild

Rural boychildren often possess a deep sense of responsibility towards their families and communities. They learn the value of hard work, resilience, and resourcefulness. However, their exposure to the broader world is limited, which can result in a narrower perspective on life's possibilities. They may hold traditional views and be less aware of modern challenges and opportunities.

Empowering the Rural Boy

To empower rural boys, it's crucial to provide access to quality education and vocational training. Mentorship programmes can expose them to a wider range of career options. Encouraging the preservation of cultural values while fostering openness to new ideas can help bridge the gap between tradition and modernity.

The Suburban Boychild: Abundance and Choices

Growing up in suburban areas offers a starkly different experience. Suburban boychildren have access to better educational institutions, healthcare, and a wider array of opportunities. They are exposed to modern technologies, diverse cultures, and a fast-paced lifestyle. However, this abundance can also lead to challenges such as materialism and distractions.

Views and Behaviours of the Suburban Boychild

Suburban boychildren often have a broader perspective on career possibilities and personal aspirations. They may experience a sense of entitlement due to their access to resources. Peer pressure and exposure to materialistic values can influence their behaviour, leading to potentially negative choices and lifestyles.

Guiding the Suburban Boychild

Guiding suburban boychildren involves instilling a sense of responsibility and gratitude. They must learn to appreciate the opportunities before them and understand the importance of making ethical choices. Mentorship programs can help them navigate the complexities of modern life while staying grounded in core values.

Creating Opportunities for Dialogue

A significant part of bridging the gap between rural and suburban boychildren involves creating opportunities for dialogue and cultural exchange. Both groups can learn from each other's strengths and challenges. This can foster empathy, broaden perspectives, and create a sense of unity among boychildren from different backgrounds.

Conclusion: Nurturing Purposeful Lives

In this chapter, we've explored the vastly different landscapes in which rural and suburban boychildren grow up. While their experiences and perspectives may differ, both have the potential to lead purposeful lives. By providing opportunities for education, mentorship, and dialogue, we can empower boychildren from all backgrounds to make choices that lead to fulfilment and purpose. Ultimately, it's not where they come from but the choices they make that define their destinies.

A Message to Teenagers

To teenagers who may be reading this, I offer some advice: It's natural to feel the pull of recklessness during these formative years, but remember that every decision you make has consequences. Seek guidance from trusted adults who genuinely care about your well-being. Educate yourself about the risks associated with reckless behaviours and understand that true strength lies in responsible choices and empathy for others.

Your teenage years are a time of self-discovery, growth, and learning. Embrace this period with an open heart and a willingness to make choices that will serve your future self. Remember that you have the power to shape your own destiny, and by making responsible decisions, you can pave the way for a brighter and more fulfilling future.

CHAPTER 32

Chapter 32

Lessons from My Father's Legacy

The Time of Plenty

During my father's lifetime, our family was fortunate to experience a period of relative abundance. He was the epitome of hard work and dedication, serving as the breadwinner and provider for our home. His unwavering commitment to his family meant that we became accustomed to having enough, and our needs were consistently met.

In those days, it was easy to take for granted the blessings of having more than enough. It fostered a sense of security and comfort that, in hindsight, concealed valuable lessons about self-sufficiency and resilience.

The Unintended Consequences

One of the unintended consequences of growing up in an environment of plenty became evident later in life. As I ventured into adulthood and faced periods of scarcity and uncertainty, I discovered that the comfort of abundance had not prepared me for the challenges of managing with less. It was a stark reminder that providing your children with more than enough can inadvertently hinder their ability to adapt to adversity.

In today's world, the role of women as working professionals has taken on increasing significance. It's a testament to the importance of financial independence and resilience in times of hardship. My father's absence due to his passing served as a poignant reminder of this reality. It underscored the need for both parents to be equipped with the skills and means to support their families.

Advice for Similar Situations

To those who find themselves in similar situations, I offer the following advice:

- **Financial Literacy:** Invest in financial literacy for yourself and your family.
- Equip your loved ones with the knowledge and skills to manage finances effectively, including budgeting and saving.
- **Embrace Self-Sufficiency:** Encourage self-sufficiency and independence among your family members. Teach them the value of hard work and resilience in the face of adversity.
- **Prepare for the unexpected:** Life is unpredictable, and it's essential to have contingency plans in place. This includes having life insurance and emergency funds to provide for your family in times of need.
- **Support Working Women:** Recognize and appreciate the importance of women as working professionals. Encourage their pursuit of financial independence and professional growth.
- **Communicate Openly:** Foster open and honest communication within your family. Discuss financial matters, goals, and plans together to ensure everyone is on the same page.

CHAPTER
33

Chapter 33

Building Resilience for the Future

Legacy and Resilience

My father's legacy continues to guide me, not only in the lessons of hard work and dedication but also in the importance of preparing for an uncertain future. His absence reinforced the need for resilience, financial independence, and a proactive approach to life's challenges.

As I navigate the complexities of adulthood, I carry with me the lessons learned from my father's time of plenty and the difficulties that followed. I understand that giving your children more than enough, while well-intentioned, may not always serve their best interests. It's the ability to adapt, to face adversity with strength and determination that truly prepares them for life's unpredictable twists and turns.

A Call to Action

In closing, I extend a call to action to those who may find themselves in similar circumstances. Recognise that your role as a parent extends beyond providing material comfort; it includes equipping your family with the tools to thrive independently. Prepare for the unexpected, encourage financial literacy, and foster resilience within your family. By doing so, you can leave a legacy that not only honours your loved ones but also empowers them to face the future with confidence and strength.

CHAPTER 34

Chapter 34

♦ *Navigating Disadvantages with Resilience*

Finding Strength in Adversity

In the wake of my father's passing, I found myself grappling with feelings of isolation and inadequacy. The disparities between my peers, who seemed to have it all, and my own circumstances weighed heavily on my sense of self-worth. It's a situation that many disadvantaged boys find themselves in, and it can be challenging to break free from the grip of self-doubt, depression, or the allure of violence.

However, I learned that adversity can be a powerful teacher, and even in the bleakest moments, there are healthy ways to cope and rise above the challenges.

Healthy Coping Mechanisms

Seek Support: Don't shoulder your burdens alone. Reach out to friends, family members, or professionals who can provide emotional support and guidance. Sharing your feelings can alleviate the weight of isolation.

Embrace Education: Education is a pathway to empowerment. Focus on your studies and set ambitious goals for yourself. Knowledge and skills can be your greatest assets in overcoming adversity.

Engage in Physical Activity: Regular exercise can have a profound impact on your mental and emotional well-being. It releases endorphins, reduces stress, and boosts self-esteem.

Connect with Mentors: Seek out role models or mentors who can offer guidance and inspiration. They can provide valuable insights and encouragement on your journey.

Practice Self-compassion: Be kind to yourself. Understand that your circumstances do not define your worth. Treat yourself with the same compassion you would offer a friend facing similar challenges.

Set Realistic Goals: Break your aspirations into smaller, achievable goals. Celebrate your victories, no matter how small, as they build your confidence and sense of accomplishment.

Engage in Creative Outlets: Art, music, writing, or any creative pursuit can be a therapeutic outlet for your emotions. Expressing yourself creatively can be healing.

Volunteer and Give Back: Helping others in need can shift your focus from your own challenges and provide a sense of purpose. It also builds a support network of like-minded individuals.

Practice Mindfulness: mindfulness and meditation techniques can help manage stress and improve mental clarity. These practises can empower you to navigate adversity with a calmer perspective.

Seek Professional Help: If feelings of self-hatred, depression, or violence persist, don't hesitate to seek professional assistance. Therapy and counselling can provide invaluable support and coping strategies.

CHAPTER 35

Chapter 35

Rising Stronger

Resilience and Transformation

In the end, my journey through isolation and adversity taught me that it's possible to rise stronger from such experiences. Disadvantage does not define your destiny; it's your response to it that matters most. By seeking support, focusing on education, nurturing self-compassion, and embracing healthy coping mechanisms, disadvantaged boys can break free from the shackles of self-hatred, depression, and violence.

Remember, resilience is not the absence of hardship but the ability to bounce back from it. Through resilience, you can turn adversity into an opportunity for growth and transformation. You have the power within you to shape a future filled with purpose, success, and well-being, regardless of the challenges you face.

CHAPTER 36

Chapter 36

The Therapeutic Power of Art

Unlocking Healing through Expression

Art, in its myriad forms, has a remarkable ability to serve as a vehicle for healing and self-expression. Whether through poetry, music, painting, or any creative outlet, it can be a refuge for those seeking solace in the face of adversity. In my own journey, I discovered the therapeutic power of art, particularly through writing poems and music.

The Poetic Voice of Healing

Writing poems became my sanctuary, a place where I could pour out my innermost thoughts and emotions. It was a means of catharsis, allowing me to release the pent-up feelings of isolation, grief, and frustration. Through poetry, I found my voice and, with it, a path towards healing.

The act of crafting words into verses became a form of self-reflection and self-acceptance. It allowed me to explore the depths of my emotions and confront the challenges I faced. It was through this process that I began to understand the power of art as a tool for emotional release and self-discovery.

The Healing Harmony of Music

Music, too, played a pivotal role in my journey. It offered a unique language through which I could communicate my inner turmoil and hopes for the future. The act of creating melodies and lyrics became an avenue for catharsis, as the vibrations of music resonated with the depths of my soul.

The healing power of music extended beyond creation. Listening to music became a source of comfort and inspiration, offering solace during moments of despair. It was a reminder that, even in the midst of adversity, there is beauty and meaning to be found.

CHAPTER 37

Chapter 37

Art as an Escape from Self-Harm

Turning to Creativity, Not Destruction

In the darkest moments of life, the urge to self-harm can be overwhelming. It's a destructive path that offers temporary relief but ultimately compounds pain and suffering. Instead, I discovered that art could serve as a constructive escape, a way to channel pain into creation rather than destruction.

Art provides a safe space to confront and process difficult emotions. Whether it's painting, writing, dancing, or any creative endeavour, it offers an alternative to self-harm. Instead of inflicting pain on ourselves, we can use art to externalise our struggles and find solace in the act of creation.

CHAPTER
38

Chapter 38

✣ *Embracing the Healing Process*

From Pain to Resilience

My journey through art as a means of healing was not without its challenges. There were moments of doubt and frustration, times when the creative process itself felt like a burden. But it was through these challenges that I learned the most valuable lesson of all—healing is a process.

Art is not a magical cure, but it is a powerful tool for transformation. It allowed me to navigate the complexities of my emotions and gradually build resilience. It taught me that healing is not linear; it's a journey of ups and downs, setbacks, and breakthroughs.

CHAPTER 39

Chapter 39

Inspiring Others Through Art

Sharing the Gift of Healing

Today, I am passionate about sharing the gift of healing through art with others who may be on their own journey to self-discovery and recovery. I've witnessed first-hand the transformative power of creative expression, and I believe it's a tool that can empower individuals to overcome even the darkest of challenges.

In this chapter, I will explore the ways in which art can be used to inspire and uplift others. From community projects to therapeutic workshops, there are countless opportunities to harness the healing potential of art and help others find their own paths to recovery.

Through art, we can offer hope, connection, and a means of transcending pain and adversity. It is my hope that this exploration of the therapeutic power of art will serve as a source of inspiration for those seeking solace, healing, and a way to escape self-harm through creativity and self-expression.

CHAPTER 40

Chapter 40

Lessons for Aspiring Men

Crafting a Path from Adversity to Adulthood

As I reflect on my journey from a disadvantaged boy to a man who has faced adversity with resilience, I've distilled a set of valuable lessons. These lessons are a guide for any young boychild who finds themselves navigating the tumultuous waters of hardship and uncertainty, seeking to emerge as a proper man.

Resilience through Adversity: Understand that adversity is not the end but a stepping stone to growth. Develop resilience by facing challenges head-on, and remember that your circumstances do not define your future.

Seek Education and Knowledge: Education is a powerful tool that can break the cycle of disadvantage. Prioritize learning and seeking knowledge from every available source.

Lean on a Support Network: Don't be afraid to seek support from family, friends, mentors, **and** professionals. You don't have to face challenges alone; others can offer guidance and encouragement.

Embrace Self-Expression: Art, in its various forms, can be a therapeutic outlet for emotions and a means of self-discovery. Explore creative avenues like writing, music, or the visual arts to express yourself.

Practice Self-Compassion: Be kind to yourself and understand that it's okay to make mistakes. Self-compassion allows you to heal and grow.

Set Goals and Work Diligently: Define clear, achievable goals for yourself and work diligently toward them. Small steps can lead to significant achievements.

Value Financial Literacy: Educate yourself about finances and budgeting. Financial literacy empowers you to make informed decisions and secure your future.

Prioritize Mental and Physical Health: Mental and physical well-being are foundational to success. Exercise regularly, seek mental health support when needed, and practise mindfulness.

Foster Healthy Relationships: Build positive, supportive relationships with family, friends, and partners. Healthy connections provide a network of emotional support.

Seek Guidance from Role Models: Look up to mentors and role models who embody the qualities you aspire to. Their guidance and insights can be invaluable.

Empower Women and Promote Equality: Recognize the importance of empowering women and promoting gender equality. A balanced partnership in life leads to stronger families and communities.

Embrace Responsibility as a Father: If you become a father, embrace the responsibilities wholeheartedly. Be present and supportive, and strive to provide a loving environment for your children.

Choose Constructive Coping Mechanisms: When faced with adversity, opt for constructive coping mechanisms like creativity, education, and seeking support, rather than destructive behaviours.

Value Resilience over Recklessness: Understand that true strength lies in resilience, not recklessness. Face challenges with courage and adaptability.

Never Stop Growing: Commit to lifelong learning and personal growth. Continuously seek opportunities to expand your knowledge and skills.

Inspire Others Through Your Journey: As you navigate your path to manhood, inspire others with your story. Share your experiences to offer hope and guidance to those facing similar struggles.

These lessons are a testament to the transformative power of determination, resilience, and the unwavering belief that, regardless of your circumstances, you have the capacity to craft a future filled with purpose, integrity, and strength.

Guidelines for Becoming a Purposeful Man

Self-Reflection: Take time to introspect and understand your values, strengths, and weaknesses. Self-awareness is the foundation of purpose.
Insight: Knowing yourself enables you to align your actions with your values, leading to a more purposeful life.
Define Your Values: Clearly define your core values. These principles will guide your decisions and actions throughout life.
Insight: When your values are clear, decision-making becomes more straightforward, and your path to purpose is more defined.
Set Meaningful Goals: Establish both short-term and long-term goals that resonate with your values. These goals give your life direction.
Insight: Purposeful men have a vision and actively work toward it through goal setting.
Cultivate Resilience: learn to bounce back from setbacks and adapt to change. Resilience is crucial for navigating life's challenges.
Insight: Resilience is not about avoiding difficulties, but about your ability to grow stronger through them.
Hone Your Skills: Continuous self-improvement is essential. Invest in education and skill development to become the best version of yourself.
Insight: Lifelong learning is the path to mastery and self-fulfilment.
Serve Others: Purpose often emerges from serving a greater good. Find ways to contribute to your community or society as a whole.
Insight: Acts of service not only benefit others but also bring a profound sense of purpose and fulfilment

Embrace Accountability: Take responsibility for your actions and decisions. Accountability is a cornerstone of integrity.

Insight: Owning your mistakes and successes alike is a mark of a purposeful man.

Foster Healthy Relationships: Build meaningful connections with family, friends, and partners. Strong relationships provide emotional support and purpose.

Insight: Your relationships reflect your values and contribute significantly to your overall sense of purpose.

Practice Gratitude: Cultivate a habit of gratitude. Appreciating what you have can lead to a more content and purposeful life.

Insight: Gratitude shifts your focus from what you lack to what you possess, fostering a sense of abundance.

Live Authentically: Be true to yourself and your values. Authenticity is the key to living a purposeful life.

Insight: Living authentically means staying true to your beliefs and not compromising your values for others.

Find Meaning in Work: Seek a career or vocation that aligns with your values and passions. Meaningful work can be a significant source of purpose.

Insight: Purposeful men are often deeply connected to their work, finding it fulfilling and aligned with their values.

Give Back: Dedicate time and resources to charitable causes. Generosity and philanthropy contribute to a sense of purpose.

Insight: Giving back allows you to be part of positive change in the world.

Practice Mindfulness: Develop mindfulness and presence in your daily life. Mindfulness can deepen your connection to your purpose.

Insight: Being fully present at the moment helps you appreciate the journey rather than just the destination.

Embrace Challenges: Don't shy away from adversity. Challenges can be opportunities for growth and a deeper understanding of your purpose.

Insight: Facing challenges with resilience can lead to personal transformation.
Learn from Failures: Instead of fearing failure, view it as a chance to learn and grow. Failure can be a stepping stone to purpose.
Insight: Purposeful men see failures as valuable experiences, not as setbacks.
Prioritize Health: Take care of your physical and mental health. A healthy body and mind enable you to pursue your purpose more effectively.
Insight: Your well-being is the foundation upon which your purpose is built.
Seek Mentors: learn from those who have walked similar paths. Mentors can provide guidance and valuable insights.
Insight: Wise mentors can accelerate your personal and professional growth.
Lead with Integrity: Integrity is the alignment of your actions with your values. Leading with integrity is a hallmark of a purposeful man.
Insight: Your character is revealed through the choices you make when no one is watching.
Inspire Others: Act as a role model and inspire others to pursue their own purpose. Your actions can create a ripple effect of positive change.
Insight: Purposeful men have a profound impact on those around them, encouraging them to find their own sense of purpose.
Practice Empathy: Cultivate empathy by seeking to understand others' perspectives and emotions. Empathy fosters compassion and connection.
Insight: Empathy strengthens relationships and can lead to a more purposeful life centred on helping others.
Stay Open to Growth: Be open to new experiences, ideas, and perspectives. Growth often occurs when you step out of your comfort zone.
Insight: A purposeful man welcomes change and sees it as an opportunity to evolve.

Manage Stress: Develop healthy stress management techniques, such as meditation or exercise. Stress can hinder your ability to pursue your purpose.

Insight: A clear mind is better equipped to identify and pursue purposeful goals.

Learn from Role Models: Study the lives of individuals who embody purpose. Their journeys can offer valuable lessons and inspiration.

Insight: Role models can provide a roadmap for your own pursuit of purpose.

Celebrate Small Wins: Acknowledge and celebrate your achievements, no matter how small. These victories can fuel your motivation and sense of purpose.

Insight: Purposeful men appreciate the progress they make along the way.

Be Patient: Understand that finding and pursuing your purpose is a lifelong journey. It may take time to fully embrace your calling.

Insight: Patience allows you to savour the process of self-discovery and growth.

Stay Humble: Humility is the recognition that you don't have all the answers. Stay open to learning from others and evolving.

Insight: A humble approach allows you to continuously refine your understanding of purpose.

Give Yourself Permission: Don't be too hard on yourself. It's okay to make mistakes and change course as you discover your purpose.

Insight: A purposeful man is compassionate toward himself as he navigates his journey.

Connect with Nature: Spend time in nature to gain perspective and reconnect with the world around you. Nature can inspire a sense of purpose.

Insight: The natural world reminds us of the interconnectedness of all life and our place within it.

Engage in Lifelong Learning: Commit to ongoing education and personal growth. Learning is a lifelong endeavour that deepens your understanding of purpose.

Insight: The pursuit of knowledge enriches your life and broadens your horizons.

Leave a Legacy: Consider the legacy you want to leave behind. What impact do you want to have on future generations? A sense of legacy can drive purpose.

Insight: Purposeful men are motivated by the knowledge that their actions today can shape a better tomorrow.

These guidelines are a roadmap for any man seeking to lead a purposeful life. They serve as reminders that purpose is not a fixed destination but a continuous path.

CHAPTER 41

Chapter 41

Building Healthy Foundations

Preparing for Love

Building successful and loving relationships starts with a strong foundation within yourself. Before you can give love, you must learn to love and understand yourself. This chapter explores the steps to creating a healthy self-concept, setting the stage for nurturing relationships.

Understanding Self-Love

The journey to healthy relationships begins with self-love. It's not a selfish act, but rather a crucial step in ensuring that you bring the best version of yourself to any partnership. Self-love involves recognising your worth, embracing your strengths, and accepting your flaws without harsh judgement.

Exploring Your Identity

To love yourself, you must first understand yourself. This involves introspection and self-discovery. Take time to explore your values, interests, and passions. What makes you unique? What are your core beliefs? Understanding your identity helps you establish your non-negotiable in relationships.

Healing Past Wounds

Many of us carry emotional baggage from past experiences, which can hinder our ability to love ourselves fully. Healing from past wounds is a vital step in building a healthy self-concept. This chapter guides you through the process of addressing past traumas and forgiving yourself for any perceived shortcomings.

Setting Boundaries

Healthy relationships require clear boundaries. This chapter emphasises the importance of setting boundaries in your personal and romantic lives. It's about defining what you will and won't tolerate and ensuring that you are respected and valued in your relationships.

Cultivating Self-Confidence

Confidence is an attractive quality in any relationship. This chapter provides practical advice on boosting your self-confidence. It's about recognising your accomplishments, setting achievable goals, and silencing that inner critic that often undermines your self-esteem.

Practicing Self-Care

Self-love extends to self-care. This chapter emphasises the significance of taking care of your physical and emotional well-being. It covers aspects like maintaining a healthy lifestyle, managing stress, and seeking professional help when needed.

Embracing Vulnerability

Being vulnerable is a key component of healthy relationships. It's about opening up, expressing your feelings, and allowing yourself to be seen, flaws and all. This chapter guides you on how to embrace vulnerability without fear.

Establishing Healthy Relationship Patterns

Once you've built a strong foundation within yourself, it's time to apply these principles to your relationships. This chapter explores how to establish healthy patterns of communication, conflict resolution, and mutual respect in your partnerships.

The Journey to love

Building a healthy self-concept is an ongoing journey, just as nurturing loving relationships is. This chapter concludes by emphasising that love is not a destination but a continuous practice. It's a journey of growth and self-discovery that ultimately enriches the relationships you cultivate.

In the pages that follow, you'll find practical advice, personal stories, and actionable steps to help you build a strong foundation within yourself, setting the stage for nurturing and successful relationships. Remember, the path to love starts from within, and with the right tools and mindset, you can create a fulfilling and loving life.

CHAPTER 42

Chapter 42

"Favour, Purpose, and the Divine Gift of Marriage"

In the intricate tapestry of life, the thread of favour weaves a path to purpose and fulfilment that often eludes us. We, the children of this modern world, often forget the profound wisdom hidden in ancient scriptures. One such wisdom, often overlooked and misunderstood, lies in the age-old saying, "He who finds a wife obtains favour from the Lord."

The pursuit of favour is an ancient and timeless quest, one that transcends generations and cultures. To understand the magnitude of this quest, we must revisit the core message embedded in this scripture. It's not merely about the act of finding a life partner, but a deeper understanding of the favour that marriage can bestow upon us.

In a world where relationships are often seen as fleeting and temporary, we've distanced ourselves from the profound significance of marriage. The truth is that a purposeful and fulfilled life is often intricately linked to the favour of the Lord, and marriage serves as a channel through which this divine favour can flow.

Unearthing the Scripture: Proverbs 18:22

The scripture that lays the foundation for this profound wisdom can be found in Proverbs 18:22: "He who finds a wife finds what is good and receives favour from the Lord." From the Old Testament of the Bible

This scripture conveys the idea that marriage, when approached with the right intent and commitment, is a blessing that can bestow the favour of the Lord. It's a journey of two souls coming together, forging a partnership that can lead to prosperity, purpose, and fulfilment.

Rediscovering the Purpose of Marriage

In our generation, the purpose of marriage has often been tainted by misconceptions and the glamorization of superficial relationships. We've lost sight of the profound meaning that marriage can bring to our lives. It's not just about sharing a home, raising children, or the blending of lives. It's about invoking the divine favour of the Lord, a favour that can guide us toward our destined purpose.

The absence of favour in our lives can lead to a sense of wandering, of feeling lost in a world of uncertainty. Without the divine favour that marriage can offer, we may find it challenging to discern our purpose and experience the fullness of life that the Lord has intended for us.

In this chapter, we journey into the profound concept of favour and how marriage, when approached with reverence and the right intentions, can serve as a conduit for the divine favour of the Lord. We'll explore how our generation's perceptions of marriage have often hindered us from experiencing the fullness of this favour and how, by understanding its profound purpose, we can unlock the gates to a life rich in fortune, purpose, and fulfilment as bestowed by the Lord God.

CHAPTER 43

Chapter 43

✣ Communication and Connection

The Art of Connection

Effective communication is at the heart of any successful relationship. In this chapter, we delve into the importance of open, honest, and empathetic communication. Learn how to actively listen, express your feelings, and connect deeply with your partner.

The Foundation of Connection

1. Open Communication

Open communication lays the groundwork for understanding and trust. Embrace transparency, sharing thoughts and experiences openly. This vulnerability fosters an environment where both partners feel secure in expressing themselves.

2. Honest Dialogue

Honesty is the bedrock of any meaningful connection. Explore the importance of truthfulness in communication, acknowledging that it builds a foundation of trust and integrity essential for a lasting relationship.

Active Listening

3. The Power of Listening

Active listening is an art that transforms mere hearing into a profound understanding. Dive into techniques that enhance your ability to attentively listen, demonstrating your genuine interest in your partner's thoughts and feelings.

4. Empathetic Responses

Empathy strengthens emotional bonds. Learn how to put yourself in your partner's shoes, acknowledging and validating their emotions. Discover the impact of empathetic responses on creating a supportive and compassionate connection.

Expressing Feelings

5. Authentic Self-Expression

Encourage the authentic expression of feelings within the relationship. Navigate the intricacies of articulating emotions, fostering an environment where both partners feel safe to share their joys, concerns, and vulnerabilities.

6. Constructive Feedback

Explore the art of providing constructive feedback. Learn to communicate concerns in a manner that promotes growth and understanding, steers clear of blame, and fosters a collaborative approach to problem-solving.

Deepening the Connection

7. Shared Experiences

Create lasting bonds through shared experiences. Whether through shared hobbies, adventures, or everyday moments, discover how shared activities contribute to a sense of togetherness and shared purpose.

8. Rituals of Connection

Explore the significance of rituals in relationships. From daily check-ins to special traditions, discover how these rituals can strengthen your bond, creating a sense of stability and continuity.

Conclusion

In conclusion, the art of connection thrives on effective communication. By embracing openness, honesty, active listening, and authentic self-expression, partners can build a foundation that fosters deep, meaningful connections. As you navigate the intricacies of human connection, remember that the journey is ongoing, and the skills developed in communication contribute to a relationship's growth and longevity.

The Foundations of Communication

This chapter begins by laying the foundations of communication within relationships. It explores the significance of communication as the bedrock upon which trust, understanding, and emotional intimacy are built. The idea that effective communication is a two-way street is emphasized, highlighting the roles of both speaking and listening.

The Foundations of Communication

This chapter begins by laying the foundations of communication within relationships. It explores the significance of communication as the bedrock upon which trust, understanding, and emotional intimacy are built. The idea that effective communication is a two-way street is emphasized, highlighting the roles of both speaking and listening.

Communication serves as the cornerstone upon which resilient relationships are constructed. In this foundational chapter, we delve into the intricacies of communication, unravelling its profound significance in shaping the bedrock of trust, understanding, and emotional intimacy between partners.

Unveiling the Core Importance
Understanding the Essence

At the heart of robust relationships lies the understanding that effective communication is not merely a conduit for conveying thoughts; it is the very essence that forges trust. We explore how clear and open communication establishes a foundation of reliability, enabling partners to feel secure in the knowledge that their words and actions align.

Transparent Expression

Building on this foundation, we navigate the role of transparent expression. Transparency becomes the mortar that binds trust, urging partners to openly share their innermost thoughts, feelings, and experiences. Here, we emphasise the transformative power of honesty as a catalyst for cultivating a relationship built on openness and trustworthiness.

Dynamics of Understanding
Two-Way Communication

Communication, we stress, is a dynamic exchange. It transcends the mere act of expressing oneself; it necessitates active engagement from both parties. We explore the concept that effective communication is a two-way street, underscoring the importance of not only articulating one's thoughts but also actively listening to the partner. This mutual dialogue becomes the nexus of shared understanding.

Non-Verbal Cues

Beyond spoken words, we unravel the intricate language of non-verbal cues. Body language, facial expressions, and gestures emerge as crucial components in the nuanced art of communication. We explore how these subtleties enrich the understanding between partners, offering insights into emotions and intentions that words alone might fail to convey.

Fostering Emotional Intimacy
Connection Beyond Words

Communication, as we delve deeper, extends beyond the realm of words. Shared experiences, shared laughter, and moments of vulnerability emerge as integral components of nurturing emotional intimacy. We explore how these shared aspects contribute to a profound connection that transcends verbal communication, weaving a tapestry of shared emotions.

Vulnerability and Authenticity

Encouraging partners to embrace vulnerability, we underscore the authenticity embedded in genuine communication. Sharing one's true self, including fears and insecurities, becomes a powerful tool for strengthening the bond. Here, authenticity acts as a bridge, fostering acceptance and understanding within the relationship.

Roles of Speaking and Listening
The Art of Speaking

In navigating the art of communication, we explore effective ways of expressing ourselves. We highlight the importance of articulating thoughts and feelings with intention, emphasising clarity and respect as vital elements in fostering constructive and open dialogue.

The Power of Listening

Turning our focus to the receptive side, we emphasise the transformative power of active listening. Genuine listening involves not just hearing words but also understanding the emotions and perspectives behind them. We provide insights into cultivating empathetic listening skills, reinforcing the idea that true communication involves an equal balance of speaking and listening.

Conclusion

In conclusion, this chapter lays the groundwork for understanding communication as more than a tool—it is the very foundation upon which successful relationships are built. By recognising its role in establishing trust, fostering understanding, and nurturing emotional intimacy, partners embark on a journey of communication that strengthens the core of their connection. Remember, effective communication is a collaborative effort that involves both speaking with intention and listening with empathy, creating a harmonious exchange that fortifies the foundations of a lasting relationship.

Active Listening

A substantial portion of the chapter is dedicated to the art of active listening. Readers are guided through techniques and strategies that foster deeper connections through listening. Real-life scenarios and examples illustrate how active listening can transform interactions, making partners feel heard and valued.

Recognizing the Significance of Active Listening
The Essence of Presence

At the core of active listening lies the essence of presence. Readers are introduced to the concept that true engagement goes beyond hearing words—it involves being fully present in the moment. We delve into the impact of focused attention on creating a space where partners feel acknowledged and respected.

Non-Verbal Cues and Body Language

Understanding that communication extends beyond verbal exchanges, this section explores the significance of non-verbal cues and body language in active listening. Real-life examples illuminate how subtle gestures and expressions can convey empathy and understanding, enriching the depth of connection between partners.

Techniques for Active Listening
Reflective Responses

Readers are guided through the power of reflective responses, illustrating how paraphrasing and summarising contribute to a more nuanced comprehension of a partner's message. Practical examples demonstrate how this technique not only confirms understanding but also encourages further expression.

Asking Clarifying Questions

This section emphasises the importance of asking clarifying questions to delve deeper into a partner's thoughts and feelings. Real-life scenarios showcase how thoughtful inquiries can unravel layers of meaning, fostering a more profound connection through active engagement.

Transformative Power in Real-Life Scenarios
Navigating Conflict Through Active Listening

Real-life examples unfold to showcase how active listening becomes a catalyst for navigating conflicts. Partners learn how to suspend judgement, tune into emotions, and respond empathetically, transforming moments of tension into opportunities for mutual understanding.

Celebrating Success Through Listening

Active listening is not confined to challenging moments; it also becomes a tool for celebrating successes. This part of the chapter illustrates how attentive listening during moments of joy and achievement reinforces the bond between partners, creating a supportive and affirming environment.

Building Deeper Connections
Empathy as a Bridge

Readers explore how empathy acts as a bridge in active listening, connecting partners on a deeper emotional level. The chapter emphasises the role of empathy in validating emotions and fostering a sense of shared experience, contributing to a more profound and meaningful connection.

Cultivating a Habit of Active Listening

The chapter concludes by guiding readers toward cultivating a habit of active listening in their daily interactions. Practical tips and insights are provided to encourage ongoing commitment, reinforcing the idea that active listening is a continuous process that enriches relationships over time.

In summary, this chapter serves as a comprehensive guide to the art of active listening. By exploring its essence, techniques, and transformative power in real-life scenarios, readers gain valuable insights into how active listening can become a cornerstone **of** building and sustaining meaningful connections within their relationships.

Expressing Feelings Honestly

Open and honest expression of feelings is another central theme. The chapter provides practical advice on how to communicate emotions authentically and respectfully. It addresses common challenges in expressing vulnerability and offers guidance on overcoming them.

Within the tapestry of relationships, the authentic expression of emotions emerges as a central theme in this chapter. Readers are guided through the intricacies of open and honest communication, gaining practical advice on how to articulate feelings authentically and respectfully. The chapter not only acknowledges the importance of expressing vulnerability but also addresses common challenges that may arise, offering valuable guidance on overcoming these hurdles.

The Importance of Authentic Expression
Creating a Safe Space

At the foundation of expressing feelings honestly lies the creation of a safe and supportive environment. The chapter begins by emphasising the significance of establishing trust within a relationship, highlighting how a secure space encourages partners to openly share their emotions without fear of judgment.

The Role of Respectful Communication

Readers are guided through the art of respectful communication, understanding that the manner in which feelings are expressed is as crucial as the expression itself. Practical advice is provided on choosing words carefully, considering the impact on the listener, and fostering a dialogue that promotes understanding and connection.

Practical Advice on Articulating Emotions
Identifying and Naming Emotions

The chapter delves into the importance of self-awareness in expressing feelings. Practical exercises guide readers in identifying and naming their emotions, laying the groundwork for clear and precise communication. This section explores how a nuanced understanding of one's feelings enhances the authenticity of expression.

Using "I" Statements

Practical techniques such as using "I" statements are explored as effective tools for expressing feelings honestly. Readers learn how framing emotions from a personal perspective fosters ownership and avoids unintentional blame, creating a conducive atmosphere for open dialogue.

Addressing Challenges in Vulnerability
Fear of Judgement

Common challenges in expressing vulnerability, such as the fear of judgement, are addressed. The chapter provides insights into understanding and overcoming this fear, empowering readers to communicate their emotions without reservation. Real-life examples illustrate the transformative power of vulnerability in strengthening connections.

Navigating Cultural and Gender Influences

Recognizing the impact of cultural and gender influences on the expression of emotions, the chapter offers nuanced guidance. Readers explore how societal expectations may shape their approach to expressing feelings and gain tools for navigating these influences while staying true to their authentic selves.

Overcoming Communication Hurdles
Active Listening as a Response

The chapter reinforces the symbiotic relationship between expressing and receiving emotions. It explores how active listening serves as a responsive tool, validating the expressed feelings and fostering a reciprocal exchange that deepens mutual understanding.

Seeking Professional Support

For challenges that extend beyond the scope of self-help, the chapter acknowledges the value of seeking professional support. Readers are encouraged to consider the assistance of therapists or counsellors as valuable resources in navigating complex emotional landscapes within relationships.

Conclusion

In conclusion, the chapter on expressing feelings honestly serves as a comprehensive guide to navigating the delicate terrain of emotional communication. By creating a safe space, offering practical advice on articulating emotions, addressing vulnerability challenges, and overcoming communication hurdles, readers gain valuable insights into fostering a relationship enriched by open and authentic expression. Remember, the journey of expressing feelings is a continuous exploration, contributing to the growth and resilience of the emotional connection within a relationship.

Conflict Resolution

Conflict is an inevitable part of any relationship. This section explores healthy ways to approach and resolve conflicts. Readers are introduced to conflict resolution strategies that prioritise understanding, compromise, and mutual respect. Real-world examples showcase the application of these strategies to resolving relationship challenges.

Within the tapestry of relationships, the authentic expression of emotions emerges as a central theme in this chapter. Readers are guided through the intricacies of open and honest communication, gaining practical advice on how to articulate feelings authentically and respectfully. The chapter not only acknowledges the importance of expressing vulnerability but also addresses common challenges that may arise, offering valuable guidance on overcoming these hurdles.

The Importance of Authentic Expression
Creating a Safe Space

At the foundation of expressing feelings honestly lies the creation of a safe and supportive environment. The chapter begins by emphasising the significance of establishing trust within a relationship, highlighting how a secure space encourages partners to openly share their emotions without fear of judgment.

Empathy and Understanding

Empathy is a cornerstone of effective communication. This chapter discusses the importance of empathy in building emotional connections. It offers insights into how readers can cultivate empathy and understand their partner's perspective, even in moments of disagreement.

CHAPTER 44

Chapter 44

Empathy and Understanding

Within the realm of effective communication, this chapter unfolds the significance of empathy as a cornerstone. Readers are immersed in an exploration of empathy's pivotal role in building profound emotional connections. The narrative not only emphasises the importance of empathy but also provides valuable insights into cultivating this essential skill, enabling readers to understand their partner's perspective, even in moments of disagreement.

Unravelling the Essence of Empathy
Defining Empathy

The chapter commences by defining empathy as more than a passive acknowledgment of another's emotions. Readers delve into the active and intentional process of understanding and sharing the feelings of their partner. The exploration begins with the recognition that empathy forms the bridge that connects individuals on a deeper emotional level.

Empathy as a Two-Way Street

Highlighting the reciprocal nature of empathy, the narrative unfolds the concept that it is a two-way street. Partners are encouraged not only to seek understanding but also to convey empathy towards each other. Real-life scenarios illustrate the transformative power of mutual empathy in forging connections.

Cultivating Empathy
Developing Emotional Intelligence

The chapter guides readers in developing emotional intelligence as a foundational skill for cultivating empathy. Exercises and reflections prompt self-awareness, allowing individuals to recognise and understand their own emotions—an essential precursor to empathetic engagement with their partners.

Active Listening as an Empathetic Tool

Building on the foundation of active listening, the narrative unfolds how this skill becomes a powerful tool for empathy. Readers learn to go beyond hearing words, tuning into the emotions and nuances underlying their partner's expressions. Practical exercises reinforce the connection between active listening and empathetic understanding.

Understanding Perspectives
Stepping into Their Shoes

Readers are encouraged to actively step into their partner's shoes, embracing the perspective-taking aspect of empathy. Through guided exercises, they navigate the complexities of seeing the world from their partner's viewpoint, fostering a deeper understanding that transcends personal biases.

Empathy in Moments of Disagreement

The chapter addresses the challenging terrain of moments of disagreement. Readers explore how empathy becomes a beacon for navigating conflicts, allowing them to connect with their partner's emotions even when opinions diverge. Practical strategies are provided to transform disagreements into opportunities for mutual understanding.

Realizing the Transformative Power
Strengthening Emotional Connections

Real-life examples illuminate the transformative power of empathy in strengthening emotional connections. Readers witness how empathetic understanding creates an environment where partners feel truly seen, heard, and valued, contributing to a resilient and flourishing relationship.

Fostering a Culture of Empathy

The chapter concludes by encouraging readers to foster a culture of empathy in their relationships. Recognizing that empathy is a skill honed over time, individuals are inspired to integrate empathetic practises into their daily interactions, creating a foundation of mutual understanding and connection.

In conclusion, the chapter on empathy and understanding serves as a comprehensive guide to enriching relationships through empathetic communication. By unravelling the essence of empathy, providing insights into cultivation, understanding perspectives, and realising its transformative power, readers embark on a journey toward deeper emotional connections. Remember, empathy is not just a skill—it is a profound expression of care and understanding that fortifies the very heart of meaningful relationships.

Non-verbal Communication

Non-verbal cues play a significant role in communication. This section delves into the subtleties of non-verbal communication, such as body language and tone of voice. It helps readers recognise and interpret these cues in themselves and their partners, enhancing their ability to communicate effectively.

Digital Communication

In the digital age, technology has transformed how we communicate. This chapter explores the impact of digital communication on relationships and offers guidance on maintaining healthy digital interactions. It addresses the common pitfalls of texting and social media and suggests strategies for using technology to enhance, rather than hinder, connection.

The Transformation of Communication in the Digital Age
Shifting Dynamics

The chapter opens by acknowledging the profound transformation technology has brought to communication. Readers are prompted to reflect on the evolution of communication in the digital age, recognising both the benefits and challenges that come with the immediacy and accessibility of digital platforms.

The Role of Technology in Relationships

Exploring the intersection of technology and relationships, the narrative emphasises how digital communication can either strengthen or strain connections. The chapter highlights the need for conscious awareness when navigating the impact of technology on the quality of interactions between partners.

Navigating Common Pitfalls
Misinterpretation in Texting

Addressing the challenges of texting, the chapter explores common pitfalls, such as misinterpretations. Readers gain insights into the limitations of text-based communication and practical strategies for mitigating misunderstandings that can arise from the absence of non-verbal cues.

The Social Media Paradox

The narrative unfolds the paradoxical nature of social media—while it provides a platform for connection, it also introduces complexities. Readers navigate the potential pitfalls of comparison, jealousy, and miscommunication that may arise within the realm of social media interactions.

Strategies for Healthy Digital Interactions
Mindful Texting

Guiding readers in cultivating mindfulness in texting, the chapter provides strategies for conveying emotions effectively through text. Techniques such as using emojis, considering tone, and being aware of context empower individuals to infuse intention and clarity into their digital messages.

Setting Boundaries in Social Media

Recognizing the importance of setting boundaries, the narrative explores how individuals can maintain a healthy balance in their social media interactions. Strategies for managing time spent on these platforms and establishing mutual expectations within the relationship are discussed.

Enhancing Connection Through Technology
Virtual Togetherness

The chapter celebrates the positive potential of technology in fostering virtual togetherness. Readers explore ways to use video calls, messaging apps, and shared online activities to strengthen their connection, especially in long-distance or busy situations.

Collaborative Digital Spaces

Encouraging collaborative engagement, the narrative explores the concept of creating digital spaces that enhance connection. Whether through shared playlists, online projects, or collaborative digital journals, partners can weave a digital tapestry that reflects shared interests and experiences.

In conclusion, the chapter on digital communication navigates the complex landscape where technology intersects with relationships. By addressing common pitfalls, offering strategies for healthy interactions, and celebrating the potential for enhanced connection through technology, readers gain valuable insights into navigating the digital age. Remember, technology is a tool, and how it shapes relationships depends on how individuals consciously engage with it. By approaching digital communication mindfully, partners can harness its potential to enrich rather than hinder their connection.

Connection Exercises

To reinforce the concepts discussed, this chapter includes practical exercises for readers to engage in with their partners. These exercises are designed to strengthen communication skills and deepen emotional connections. They encourage partners to explore each other's thoughts, feelings, and desires in a safe and nurturing environment.

This chapter serves as a practical guide, offering readers a collection of exercises meticulously designed to reinforce the concepts explored in earlier chapters. With a focus on enhancing communication skills and deepening emotional connections, these exercises encourage partners to actively engage in the exploration of each other's thoughts, feelings, and desires within a safe and nurturing environment.

Building a Foundation of Connection
Exercise 1: Shared Journaling

The chapter opens with a collaborative exercise in shared journaling. Partners are encouraged to maintain a shared digital or physical journal where they can express thoughts, feelings, and reflections. This exercise fosters a sense of intimacy through the written word and provides a space for open and ongoing communication.

Exercise 2: Weekly Check-Ins

Readers are introduced to the concept of weekly check-ins—a structured yet flexible exercise where partners set aside time to discuss their highs, lows, and any challenges they may be facing. This regular practise reinforces the habit of active listening and creates a dedicated space for sharing and understanding.

Enhancing Communication Skills
Exercise 3: Mirror Listening

Partners engage in mirror listening, a reflective exercise where one person expresses a thought or feeling, and the other paraphrases or mirrors back what they heard. This exercise not only strengthens the speaker's feeling of being heard but also hones the listener's active listening skills.

Exercise 4: Perspective-Sharing Game

The chapter introduces a perspective-sharing game where partners take turns sharing their perspectives on various topics or scenarios. This interactive exercise promotes understanding and empathy as partners explore each other's viewpoints, fostering a deeper connection through shared insights.

Deepening Emotional Connections
Exercise 5: Emotion Charades

A playful yet profound exercise, emotion charades involve the non-verbal expression of emotions. Partners take turns acting out different emotions, prompting the other to guess. This dynamic activity enhances emotional intelligence, allowing partners to connect on a visceral level.

Exercise 6: Dream Mapping

Dream mapping invites partners to visually represent their individual and shared dreams. Using images, words, or symbols, they create a map that illustrates their aspirations. This exercise not only deepens understanding but also aligns partners with their visions for the future.

Nurturing a Safe Environment
Exercise 7: Vulnerability Ritual

To address the challenge of expressing vulnerability, partners engage in a vulnerability ritual. This exercise involves setting aside time to share something personal and vulnerable. Partners take turns, creating a ritual that fosters a safe and supportive environment for open expression.

Exercise 8: Appreciation Exchange

The chapter concludes with an appreciation exchange exercise, where partners take turns expressing genuine appreciation for each other. This positive and affirming practise reinforces a culture of gratitude within the relationship, strengthening the emotional connection.

In conclusion, the chapter on connection exercises offers readers a practical roadmap to actively apply the concepts discussed. By engaging in these exercises, partners not only reinforce their communication skills but also create a space for meaningful exploration and connection. Remember, these exercises are tools—how partners utilise them in their unique relationship journey contributes to the ongoing growth and depth of their connection.

Conclusion: Nurturing Bonds through Communication

The chapter concludes by highlighting the transformative power of effective communication in nurturing bonds between partners. It reinforces the idea that the art of connection is an ongoing practise that requires effort and mindfulness. Readers are encouraged to apply the principles discussed to enhance their relationships, fostering deeper connections built on trust, understanding, and empathy.

Discover valuable insights and practical tools to master the art of connection through communication. By embracing these principles, you can create and sustain relationships that are rooted in mutual respect, emotional intimacy, and lasting love.

CHAPTER 45

Chapter 45

✦ *The Cornerstones of Love*

Trust and respect are non-negotiable in any loving relationship. Explore the dynamics of trust and how to build and maintain it. Understand the value of respecting boundaries and individuality with your partner.

Trust and Respect: The Cornerstones of Love

Trust and respect are non-negotiable in any loving relationship. Explore the dynamics of trust and how to build and maintain it. Understand the value of respecting boundaries and individuality in your partner.

The Importance of Trust in Love

This chapter opens with an exploration of trust as the foundation upon which love is built. It emphasises that trust is not only about fidelity but also about reliability, consistency, and emotional safety. Real-life stories illustrate how trust can be both fragile and resilient in relationships.

Building Trust

Readers are guided through the process of building trust within a relationship. This includes open and honest communication, consistency in actions, and demonstrating reliability over time. The chapter offers practical tips and exercises for nurturing trust between partners.

The Role of Respect

Respect is closely intertwined with trust. The chapter delves into the significance of respecting each other's boundaries, values, and individuality. It discusses how mutual respect fosters a sense of equality and appreciation within the relationship.

Boundary Setting and Respect

Setting and respecting boundaries is a key aspect of maintaining trust and respect. This section explores the importance of clear communication when establishing boundaries and the significance of honouring each other's limits. Readers learn how to navigate boundary discussions with sensitivity and empathy.

Rebuilding Trust After Betrayal

In some cases, trust may be compromised due to betrayal or broken promises. This chapter provides guidance on the challenging journey of rebuilding trust after such incidents. It outlines steps for acknowledging mistakes, making amends, and gradually rebuilding a sense of security.

Respecting Differences

Every individual is unique, and respecting these differences is essential in a loving relationship. This section encourages readers to celebrate their partner's distinct qualities and interests. It discusses how acknowledging and valuing these differences can strengthen the bond.

The Role of Vulnerability

Vulnerability is a theme revisited in the context of trust and respect. The chapter highlights how being vulnerable with your partner can deepen the connection and foster trust. It offers insights into how to share vulnerabilities without fear of judgment.

Case Studies and Real-Life Scenarios

Throughout the chapter, case studies and real-life scenarios are presented to illustrate the concepts discussed. These stories provide relatable examples of trust and respect dynamics in various relationship contexts, offering insights and lessons learned.

Conclusion: Nurturing Love Through Trust and Respect

The chapter concludes by emphasising that trust and respect are ongoing commitments within a relationship. It underscores that they are not only the cornerstones of love but also the pillars that support a lasting and fulfilling partnership. Readers are encouraged to reflect on their own relationships and consider how they can cultivate trust and respect to deepen their love.

Explore the intricate dynamics of trust and respect, gaining valuable insights and practical tools for nurturing these essential components of love. By embracing these principles, you can create a relationship that thrives on a foundation of trust, mutual respect, and enduring love.

CHAPTER 46

Chapter 46

Conflict Resolution and Growth

Navigating Stormy Waters

Conflict is a natural part of any relationship. This chapter guides you through healthy conflict resolution techniques and strategies for personal growth through challenges. Discover how conflicts can strengthen your bond rather than weaken it.

Conflict Resolution and Growth: Navigating Stormy Waters

Conflict is a natural part of any relationship. This chapter guides you through healthy conflict resolution techniques and strategies for personal growth through challenges. Discover how conflicts can strengthen your bond rather than weaken it.

The Role of Conflict in Relationships

This chapter begins by acknowledging that conflict is not a sign of a failing relationship but a natural consequence of two unique individuals coming together. It emphasises that conflicts, when handled constructively, can lead to growth and a deeper understanding of each other.

Understanding the Nature of Conflict

Readers are encouraged to explore the different types of conflicts that can arise in relationships, from disagreements over values to communication breakdowns. Understanding the root causes of conflicts is the first step in addressing them effectively.

Healthy Conflict Resolution Strategies

The heart of the chapter is dedicated to practical conflict resolution strategies. These include active listening, empathy, using "I" statements to express feelings, and finding common ground. Case studies and scenarios illustrate how these strategies can be applied in real-life situations.

The Power of Effective Communication

Effective communication is highlighted as a crucial element in resolving conflicts. This section explores how clear and respectful communication can prevent misunderstandings and de-escalate tensions. It provides guidance on how to create a safe space for open dialogue.

Forgiveness and Healing

After conflicts, forgiveness and healing play a vital role in moving forward. This chapter discusses the importance of forgiving both yourself and your partner, as well as seeking forgiveness when needed. It explores the process of healing emotional wounds caused by conflicts.

Conflict as a Catalyst for Growth

A significant theme is the idea that conflicts can be catalysts for personal and relational growth. It emphasises that navigating challenges together can strengthen the bond between partners. The chapter provides insights into how conflicts can lead to greater resilience and understanding.

Conflict Prevention and Resolution in the Long Term

The chapter also addresses long-term conflict prevention and resolution. It discusses how to establish healthy patterns of communication and conflict resolution in the relationship. Readers are encouraged to reflect on their own conflict styles and consider how they can evolve them for the better.

Case Studies and Real-Life Scenarios

Throughout the chapter, case studies and real-life scenarios are presented to illustrate the concepts discussed. These stories provide relatable examples of conflicts in relationships and how they can be resolved and used for growth.

Case Study 1: The Journey to Rebuilding Trust After Betrayal

Scenario:
John and Mary faced a significant breach of trust when John's previous relationship ended due to infidelity. This history of betrayal casts a shadow on their new relationship. Mary struggled with insecurity, while John found it challenging to regain trust. Through open conversations, counselling, and John's consistent efforts to demonstrate loyalty, they navigated the complex path of rebuilding trust. This journey became a testament to the resilience of love when confronted with the ghosts of past relationships.

Lesson Learned:

Rebuilding trust requires time, open communication, and sincere efforts to address the scars left by past betrayals. A commitment to growth and healing can lead to a stronger, more resilient bond.

Case Study 2: Bridging Cultural Divides for Lasting Harmony

Scenario:
Sarah and David hail from different cultural backgrounds, contributing to misunderstandings and clashes in their relationship. Drawing parallels with a past relationship that failed due to cultural differences, they decided to actively educate themselves about each other's cultural nuances. By embracing diversity, learning together, and fostering a genuine appreciation for their unique backgrounds, they turned potential pitfalls into sources of strength.

Lesson Learned:
Acknowledging and celebrating cultural differences can enhance relationship dynamics. The willingness to learn and adapt cultivates a sense of unity and shared understanding.

Real-Life Scenario: Transforming Co-Parenting Challenges into Collaborative Growth

Scenario:
Reflecting on challenges from a previous relationship where co-parenting was marred by conflicts, Mark and Lisa realised the importance of effective communication for successful co-parenting. By establishing clear boundaries, setting shared goals for their child's well-being, and prioritising open dialogue, they transformed their co-parenting dynamic. The lessons learned from past struggles became the catalyst for building a more cooperative and supportive co-parenting relationship.

Lesson Learned:
Co-parenting challenges can be transformed through effective communication, shared goals, and a commitment to prioritising the child's well-being. Past difficulties can serve as valuable lessons for shaping a more collaborative future.

These case studies and scenarios illustrate the transformative power of applying lessons from past relationships to navigate current challenges. Through open communication, understanding, and a commitment to growth, couples can turn potential pitfalls into opportunities for building stronger, more harmonious relationships.

Conclusion: Navigating Stormy Waters Together

The chapter concludes by highlighting that conflicts are not roadblocks but opportunities for growth. It reinforces the idea that healthy conflict resolution can deepen the connection between partners and lead to a more resilient and enduring relationship. Readers are encouraged to embrace conflicts as part of the journey and to apply the strategies discussed to navigate them successfully.

Discover practical techniques for resolving conflicts and leveraging them as opportunities for personal and relational growth. By approaching conflicts with empathy, effective communication, and a growth mindset, you can build a relationship that thrives through life's challenges.

CHAPTER 47

Chapter 47

Nurturing Lifelong Love

The Journey Continues

In the final chapter, we explore the keys to nurturing lifelong love. Learn how to keep the flame of passion alive, grow together as individuals, and continue building a relationship that stands the test of time.

These chapters offer insights, advice, and practical steps to help disadvantaged boys build successful, loving, and non-abusive relationships that prioritise the safety and security of all parties involved.

Chapter Title: "Misconceptions of Independence: Nurturing Love and Success"

CHAPTER 48

Chapter 48

✦ *Breaking the Chains of Misconception*

Independence, a word often revered and sought after, can be both a beacon of hope and a source of misconception. In this chapter, we unravel the common misconceptions that surround the concept of independence, shedding light on the truths that lie beneath. We explore the idea that independence is not synonymous with isolation, that it need not be a lonely path, and that it can be achieved without leaving love and relationships in its wake. It's a chapter that challenges preconceived notions and invites readers to rethink the essence of true independence.

CHAPTER 49

Chapter 49

Lessons in Love and Interdependence

The pursuit of independence is a journey filled with valuable lessons, and one of the most important is the discovery of interdependence. In this chapter, we delve into the concept of interdependence, emphasising that being self-sufficient doesn't mean going it alone. We explore the power of partnerships, the beauty of shared responsibilities, and the strength that comes from leaning on one another. It's a lesson in love and connection, one that teaches us that while we strive for personal success, we can also nurture relationships that thrive.

CHAPTER 50

Chapter 50

Independence and Beyond: Success without Disadvantage

As we conclude our exploration of independence, we shift our focus to the idea of success without disadvantage. In this chapter, we reflect on the lessons learned on the path to independence and consider how they can be harnessed to pave the way for a future that is both self-sustaining and nurturing of love and relationships. We examine the importance of balancing personal achievement with a commitment to those we hold dear. It's a chapter that provides a roadmap for those who aspire to rise above adversity, dispelling the myths of disadvantage and showing that true success is not achieved at the expense of love and connection.

These three chapters form a narrative that encourages readers to re-evaluate their perceptions of independence, guiding them towards a balanced life filled with success, love, and the knowledge that they need not be disadvantaged on their journey to personal achievement.

CHAPTER 51

Chapter 51

♦ *Breaking the Chains of Misconception*

Misconception 1: Independence Equals Isolation

Truth: Independence doesn't mean cutting off ties; it means self-sufficiency.
Practical Application: Embrace your independence while nurturing relationships. Seek balance by setting boundaries and allocating time for loved ones. Make communication a priority.

Misconception 2: Dependence Equals Weakness

Truth: Interdependence fosters strength through collaboration.
Practical Application: Acknowledge that depending on others isn't a sign of weakness. Celebrate strengths and complement each other. Encourage teamwork in personal and professional life.

Misconception 3: Independence Excludes Vulnerability

Truth: True independence embraces vulnerability and growth.
Practical Application: Embrace vulnerability as a source of strength. Be open about your fears and doubts. Seek guidance from mentors and learn from shared experiences.

CHAPTER 52

Chapter 52

Lessons in Love and Interdependence

The Power of Partnerships

Truth: A strong partnership enhances your independence.
Practical Application: Choose partners who support your goals and share your values. Foster a collaborative spirit in your personal and professional lives.

The Beauty of Shared Responsibilities

Truth: Sharing responsibilities nurtures your relationships.
Practical Application: Recognize that you don't have to do everything alone. Allocate tasks and responsibilities in a fair and considerate manner.

Strength in Leaning on One Another

Truth: Interdependence is about mutual support.
Practical Application: Lean on your partner, friends, and family when you need assistance. Create an environment where seeking help is encouraged.

CHAPTER 53

Chapter 53

Independence and Beyond: Success Without Disadvantage

Independence and Beyond: Success Without Disadvantage

Balancing Personal Achievement and Relationships

Truth: Personal success can coexist with love and connection.
Practical Application: Prioritize your goals while being mindful of your relationships. Communicate your aspirations and involve your loved ones in your journey.

Rising Above Adversity

Truth: Disadvantages can be overcome through resilience and support.
Practical Application: Face adversity with determination and seek guidance from mentors and peers. Build a network that uplifts you.

Dispelling Myths of Disadvantage

Truth: Success is not achieved at the expense of love and connection.
Practical Application: Live your life in a way that disproves the myths. Strive for success, nurturing love and support along the way.

These practical applications provide guidance on how to implement the truths revealed in the chapters, ensuring that the pursuit of independence and success doesn't lead to the disadvantage of love and relationships but rather creates a harmonious and fulfilling life.

CHAPTER 54

Chapter 54

"Nurturing True Love and Success: My Journey"

In a world filled with uncertainties and challenges, my story as a disadvantaged boychild mirrors the experiences of many others who, like me, didn't receive proper guidance on what it means to be a man. Raised in an environment that lacked positive role models, I faced the dilemma of navigating the complex landscape of relationships, particularly with the opposite sex.

The Early Confusion: Toxic Traits Mistaken for Masculinity

As I ventured into the world of relationships, I initially grappled with misconceptions about masculinity. I witnessed negative traits like aggression, emotional suppression, and dominance being mistakenly perceived as signs of manhood. Confused by these harmful stereotypes, I struggled to form healthy connections with the opposite sex.

The Turning Point: A Quest for Knowledge and Growth

Aware that I needed to break free from these toxic patterns, I embarked on a journey of self-discovery. I recognised the importance of educating myself about true masculinity and the art of building meaningful relationships. This quest for knowledge led me to books, mentors, and support networks that could guide me toward a healthier, more balanced approach.

Learning to Communicate: The Foundation of Healthy Relationships

One pivotal lesson I embraced was the art of communication. I realised that effective communication was the cornerstone of any successful relationship. Learning to express my feelings honestly and to actively listen to the needs and concerns of my partner proved to be transformative. It allowed me to break down emotional barriers and build connections based on trust and understanding.

Respect and Equality: The Bedrock of Love

Understanding the importance of respect and equality was another significant step in my journey. I grasped that genuine love wasn't about asserting dominance or control but about respecting individual boundaries and valuing the autonomy of my partner. In doing so, I nurtured **a** love that was built on mutual admiration and support.

Navigating Conflict with Grace: A Path to Growth

In any relationship, conflicts are inevitable, and I learned the importance of navigating them with grace. I discovered that disagreements, when handled with respect and empathy, could strengthen the bond rather than weaken it. Conflict resolution became an opportunity for personal and relational growth.

The Present and the Future: A Portrait of True Love and Success

As I continued on my path of growth and self-discovery, I emerged as a man who embodied the essence of true love and success. My relationships were built on respect, trust, and open communication. I had learned that masculinity didn't lie in dominance but in kindness, empathy, and the ability to nurture meaningful connections.

This chapter tells the story of my evolution from confusion and toxic traits to a mature understanding of true love and success. It reflects the possibility of growth and transformation, highlighting that the disadvantaged can rise above stereotypes and learn to interact with the opposite sex in a healthy, nurturing, and respectful manner.

CHAPTER 55

Chapter 55

✠ The Weight of Generational Curses

Breaking the Chains of the Past

In the opening chapter of "From Adversity to Purpose: Nurturing Love and Success," K. Daniel Selapa delves deep into the concept of generational curses. He paints a vivid picture of how these burdens, often rooted in family history, can cast a long shadow over our lives. The weight of generational curses can manifest in various ways, from financial struggles to dysfunctional relationships. Selapa shares his own experiences growing up in such circumstances, emphasising that generational curses are not an inheritance but a challenge to overcome.

Finding Spiritual Resilience
A Foundation of Faith

Selapa's journey towards breaking free from generational curses begins with spirituality. Chapter 2 explores the role of faith in transcending the limitations imposed by the past. He shares how embracing a spiritual path provided him with the strength to rise above his circumstances. Readers are encouraged to connect with their faith, whatever form it may take, as a powerful means of finding resilience in the face of adversity.

The Hard Work of Transformation
Shaping a New Destiny

Breaking free from generational curses demands hard work and determination. In this chapter, Selapa delves into the importance of diligence and perseverance. He shares personal anecdotes of his own efforts to rise above adversity through education and skill development. The message is clear: hard work is a critical component of rewriting one's family legacy.

: Offering God Something to Use
Transcending the Past through Purpose

Selapa believes that offering God something to use is a key step in breaking free from generational curses. This chapter explores the idea that by discovering and living our purpose, we become instruments for positive change in our families and communities. Readers are encouraged to seek their unique calling, using their skills and passions to make a positive impact. Selapa reminds us that purpose can be a beacon of light, illuminating the path to a brighter future for ourselves and generations to come.

Guidance for Breaking Generational Curses

Throughout these chapters, Selapa provides readers with guidance on breaking free from generational curses:
Recognize the Patterns: The first step is acknowledging the existence of generational curses in your life and identifying the recurring patterns that need to be broken.
Embrace Spirituality: Connect with your spiritual beliefs and find strength, guidance, and solace in your faith.
Commit to Hard Work: Understand that breaking generational curses requires effort and dedication. Invest in your education, skills, and personal development.
Discover Your Purpose: Seek your life's purpose and use your talents and passions to create a positive impact. By offering God something to use, you become a catalyst for change.

Seek Support: Don't hesitate to seek support from mentors, counsellors, or a supportive community. You don't have to face this journey alone.

By combining spirituality, hard work, and purpose, you can shatter the chains of generational curses and pave the way for a brighter, more purposeful future.

Chapter: The Weight of Generational Curses

In this chapter, K. Daniel Selapa offers a profound message of hope to those burdened by generational curses. He begins by emphasising that these curses need not define our destinies. By recognising them as challenges to overcome rather than inevitable fates, we can take the first step toward liberation. Selapa encourages readers to explore their family histories, identify patterns, and confront the negative influences that have held them back.

He advises that a crucial aspect of breaking free from generational curses lies in self-awareness. By understanding the ways these curses have affected our lives, we can make conscious choices to defy their impact. This chapter serves as a reminder that liberation starts within, by shifting our mindset from victimhood to empowerment.

Finding Spiritual Resilience

Selapa's exploration of spirituality as a means to transcend generational curses is deeply insightful. He encourages readers to tap into their spiritual beliefs, whatever form they may take, to find strength and guidance. This chapter is a guide for those seeking a spiritual foundation to help them weather life's storms.

He discusses the importance of prayer, meditation, or any spiritual practise that connects us to a higher power. These practises can provide solace during difficult times and serve as a source of resilience. Selapa's message is clear: faith can be a powerful force in breaking the chains of generational curses.

: The Hard Work of Transformation

Selapa underscores the significance of diligence and determination in breaking free from generational curses. He shares personal anecdotes of his journey, demonstrating that hard work is a critical component of rewriting one's family legacy. In this chapter, readers are reminded that their destinies are not predetermined but can be shaped through effort and perseverance.

He advises individuals to invest in education, skill development, and personal growth. By acquiring knowledge and honing their abilities, they can create opportunities that were previously out of reach. This chapter serves as a motivational guide, urging readers to believe in their capacity for change and to take tangible steps towards a brighter future.

: Offering God Something to Use

In this chapter, Selapa explores the concept of purpose as a means of transcending generational curses. He believes that by discovering and living one's purpose, individuals become instruments for positive change in their families and communities. Readers are encouraged to seek their unique calling and utilise their skills and passions to make a positive impact.

Selapa's message is clear: purpose can be a transformative force, illuminating the path to a brighter future. He advises readers to reflect on their passions, talents, and values to uncover their purpose. By doing so, they can find a sense of direction and fulfilment that propels them beyond the limitations of their past.

Throughout these chapters, Selapa's guidance serves as a roadmap for those seeking to break free from generational curses. By recognising these challenges, embracing spirituality, working diligently, and discovering their purpose, individuals can pave the way to a future defined by success, purpose, and fulfilment.

Conclusion: The Path to Love and Purpose

In the pages of this book, we have embarked on a transformative journey, exploring the profound essence of becoming purposeful men and nurturing loving, respectful relationships. From the trials of adversity to the joys of self-discovery, each chapter has unveiled a valuable lesson in the pursuit of a meaningful life.

As disadvantaged boys, you have faced challenges that have tested your resilience, but you have also discovered the boundless potential within you. You've learned that adversity is not your inheritance but a stepping stone to growth. Through education, resilience, and an unwavering belief in your abilities, you can overcome any obstacle.

In the realm of relationships, you have unearthed the principles that build strong foundations for love and partnership. You've seen that love should never be tainted by abuse or violence, but rather should be nurtured through communication, trust, respect, and growth.

Remember, your journey is not defined by your circumstances, but by the choices you make and the values you hold dear. Embrace your purpose, strive for personal growth, and aspire to be the best version of yourselves. As you navigate life's challenges, stay true to your principles, cherish your relationships, and never stop learning.

In closing, I leave you with this impactful message: You are the architects of your destiny, and your potential is limitless. The world is waiting for the purposeful men you are destined to become. Embrace the journey with courage, compassion, and unwavering determination. Your legacy will inspire generations to come, and your love will transform lives.

CHAPTER 56

Chapter 56

Failure Is Not My Inheritance

Failure Is Not My Inheritance, I refuse
This is my firm belief.
I believe I was born into greatness. Not into hopelessness
I say this with love and great respect for me.
I may not have fancy clothes and money in my pocket.
There is more to life than fancy things, with or without material things.
I can be whatever I want to be, despite family experience.
I am destined for victory.
I may not have friends or relatives, but that would not steal my joy or opportunities for success.
I may not have an exact date of birth or have never celebrated a birthday.
There is more to life than birthdays.
My time will come.
It is my time to arise and shine.
Nomakanjane ! Lege bakareng!
Failure Is Not My Inheritance
And I will not embrace it.
I hate failure with all my heart.
I believe in the beauty of my dreams.
And my family is looking forward to a brighter tomorrow.
Failure will not rob me of my future.
I believe I can. Yes, yes, I can.
This land is too long for me.
The future is awaiting my embrace as the future president.
Whether I am from Ga-malebogo or Spoko Park
Whether I woke up in a shack or a two-room house

My future will be far better than my current situation.
I am a leader! A hard worker! A head, not a tail!
Ke ikgantsha kanna!

Biography of the Author

Kamogelo Daniel Selapa, a visionary at the age of 24, is a multifaceted professional making waves in both the literary and business worlds. As an accomplished author, he captivates audiences with his insightful writings, offering a fresh perspective on various subjects.Beyond his literary pursuits,  Kamogelo serves as the Managing Director of Link To Emerge International, a role in which he demonstrates exceptional leadership and strategic vision. He also brings his expertise to the forefront as the Training Manager for Lee and Dee Consulting and Training Services, where he excels in imparting knowledge and empowering individuals to reach their full potential.Driven by a passion for continuous learning and professional development, Kamogelo is currently pursuing an Executive Diploma in Procurement and Project Management at UniAnthena, further enhancing his skills and expertise in the field.Hailing from the vibrant community of Seshego Zone 8, Kamogelo's roots serve as a constant source of inspiration, grounding him in his values and guiding his ambitions.In his leisure time, Kamogelo immerses himself in the world of literature, finding solace and enlightenment within the pages of books. He also actively engages in business events and networking activities, seizing every opportunity to stay abreast of emerging industry trends and forge valuable connections.With a relentless drive for success and a commitment to excellence, Kamogelo Daniel Selapa is a force to be reckoned with, leaving an indelible mark on both the literary and business landscapes.

www.ingramcontent.com/pod-product-compliance
Lightning Source LLC
Chambersburg PA
CBHW041608220426
43667CB00001B/1